S. Hrg. 114–314

RUSSIAN STRATEGY AND MILITARY OPERATIONS

HEARING

BEFORE THE

COMMITTEE ON ARMED SERVICES
UNITED STATES SENATE

ONE HUNDRED FOURTEENTH CONGRESS

FIRST SESSION

OCTOBER 8, 2015

Printed for the use of the Committee on Armed Services

Available via the World Wide Web: http://www.fdsys.gov/

U.S. GOVERNMENT PUBLISHING OFFICE

20–922 PDF   WASHINGTON : 2016

For sale by the Superintendent of Documents, U.S. Government Publishing Office
Internet: bookstore.gpo.gov   Phone: toll free (866) 512–1800; DC area (202) 512–1800
Fax: (202) 512–2104   Mail: Stop IDCC, Washington, DC 20402–0001

COMMITTEE ON ARMED SERVICES

JOHN McCAIN, Arizona, *Chairman*

JAMES M. INHOFE, Oklahoma
JEFF SESSIONS, Alabama
ROGER F. WICKER, Mississippi
KELLY AYOTTE, New Hampshire
DEB FISCHER, Nebraska
TOM COTTON, Arkansas
MIKE ROUNDS, South Dakota
JONI ERNST, Iowa
THOM TILLIS, North Carolina
DAN SULLIVAN, Alaska
MIKE LEE, Utah
LINDSEY GRAHAM, South Carolina
TED CRUZ, Texas

JACK REED, Rhode Island
BILL NELSON, Florida
CLAIRE McCASKILL, Missouri
JOE MANCHIN III, West Virginia
JEANNE SHAHEEN, New Hampshire
KIRSTEN E. GILLIBRAND, New York
RICHARD BLUMENTHAL, Connecticut
JOE DONNELLY, Indiana
MAZIE K. HIRONO, Hawaii
TIM KAINE, Virginia
ANGUS S. KING, JR., Maine
MARTIN HEINRICH, New Mexico

CHRISTIAN D. BROSE, *Staff Director*
ELIZABETH L. KING, *Minority Staff Director*

(II)

CONTENTS

OCTOBER 8, 2015

Page

RUSSIAN STRATEGY AND MILITARY OPERATIONS 1
Keane, General John M., USA (Ret.), Chairman, Institute for the Study
    of War and Former Vice Chief of Staff of the Army 5
Conley, Heather, Senior Vice President for Europe, Eurasia, and the Arctic;
    Director, Europe Program, Center for Strategic and International Studies ... 14
Sestanovich, Hon. Stephen, George F. Kennan Senior Fellow for Russian
    and Eurasian Studies, Council on Foreign Relations, Columbia University .. 24
Jones, General James L., USMC (Ret.), Chairman, Brent Scowcroft Center
    on International Security, Atlantic Council, and Former National Security
    Advisor 28

(III)

RUSSIAN STRATEGY AND MILITARY OPERATIONS

THURSDAY, OCTOBER 8, 2015

U.S. SENATE,
COMMITTEE ON ARMED SERVICES,
Washington, DC.

The committee met, pursuant to notice, at 9:30 a.m. in Room SH–216, Hart Senate Office Building, Senator John McCain (chairman) presiding.

Committee members present: Senators McCain, Inhofe, Sessions, Wicker, Ayotte, Fischer, Cotton, Rounds, Ernst, Tillis, Sullivan, Lee, Reed, McCaskill, Manchin, Gillibrand, Blumenthal, Donnelly, Hirono, King, and Heinrich.

OPENING STATEMENT OF SENATOR JOHN McCAIN, CHAIRMAN

Senator McCAIN. Well, good morning. The Senate Armed Services Committee meets this morning to receive testimony on Russian Strategy and Military Operations, obviously a pretty important time to have this discussion.

I'd like to thank our distinguished panel of witnesses for appearing before us today: General Jack Keane, of the Institute for the Study of War; General James Jones, of the Atlantic Council; Ms. Heather Conley, of the Center for Strategic and International Studies; and Dr. Stephen Sestanovich, of the Council on Foreign Relations. A very distinguished panel.

Last year, Vladimir Putin's invasion of Ukraine and annexation of Crimea forced a recognition, for anyone who is not yet convinced, that we're confronting a challenge that many had assumed was resigned to the history books, a strong militarily capable Russia that is hostile to our interests and our values, and seeks to challenge the international order that American leaders of both parties have sought to maintain since the end of World War II.

Today, Russia continues to destabilize Ukraine and menace our NATO allies in Europe with aggressive military behavior. For more than a year, an overwhelming bipartisan majority in Congress, as well as many of the President's top advisors, have warned that failure to offer greater support to Ukraine, especially defensive lethal assistance, would send a message of weakness that would invite the very aggression we seek to avoid. Unfortunately, this is what has happened. As the old saying goes, Mr. Putin's appetite is growing with the eating.

Now, in a profound echo of the Cold War, Russia has intervened militarily in Syria on behalf of the murderous regime of Bashar al-Assad. Just consider how historically unprecedented this is. In all of its Soviet and post-Soviet history, Russia never intervened overtly militarily beyond its so-called near abroad. Now Vladimir Putin is doing so, and it has become the latest disastrous turn in the Middle East as well as another humiliating setback for the United States.

As in past crises, however, the White House is once again floundering. Just consider: A few weeks ago, the administration warned Russia not to send its forces to Syria. Russia did it anyway. The administration then tried to block Russia's access to airspace en route to Syria. It failed. The consequence? U.S. defense officials rushed into talks with Russia's military to, quote, ''deconflict'' in Syria. Our Secretary of State called Russia's actions an, quote, ''opportunity to cooperate'' because we share, quote, ''fundamental principles.'' And President Obama acquiesced to his first formal meeting in 2 years with Vladimir Putin, undermining international efforts, post-Crimea, to isolate Russia, exactly as Putin desired. And how did Putin respond? By bombing U.S.-backed opposition groups in Syria.

President Obama is fond of saying there is no military solution to this or any other crisis. This ignores the reality that there is a major military dimension to the problem. And it's getting worse each day. It also ignores history. Most civil wars actually do end when one side wins and the other side loses. That is Putin's military solution, and he is now imposing it with Russian airpower in an anti-American coalition of Syrian, Iranian, Hezbollah ground forces. We should expect Russian troops to take the field with them. We should also not be surprised if Putin expands his anti-American coalition's operations into Iraq, where they have already established an intelligence partnership with Baghdad.

However this conflict ends, it must not involve Vladimir Putin shoring up his partners, crushing ours, destroying our remaining credibility in the Middle East, and restoring Russia as a major power in this vital region, as Putin wants. We cannot shy away from confronting Russia in Syria, as Putin expects. His intervention has raised the costs and risks of greater U.S. involvement in Syria, but it has not negated the steps we must take. Indeed, it has made them more necessary, not least because Putin's actions will influence every aspect of this conflict: the refugee crisis, the mass atrocities, and the growth of ISIL.

As everyone from David Petraeus to Hillary Clinton has advocated, we must rally an international coalition to establish enclaves in Syria to protect civilians and our moderate partners, and do what is necessary to defend them. If Assad continues to barrel-bomb civilians, we should destroy his air force's ability to operate. And if Russia continues to attack our opposition partners, we must impose greater costs on Russia's interests; for example, by striking meaningful Syrian regime targets.

But, we should not confine our response to Syria. We must look to impose costs on Russia more broadly, including the provision of arms to Ukraine, the increase of targeted sanctions, and steps to deepen Russia's international isolation.

We must also recognize the growing challenge that Russia poses in other areas and domains. According to public reports, Russian actors are behind a growing and increasing blatant campaign of cyberattacks against the United States, including the recent attack on the Joint Staff at the Department of Defense. Along the eastern flank of NATO, Russia is moving back into old military bases it abandoned long ago and deploying growing numbers of its modernized military forces, especially anti-access and area-denial weapons designed specifically to counter the United States in asymmetric ways.

Russia's challenge even extends to the Arctic region, where Russia is involved in a significant military buildup of its air, ground, and naval forces, and has recently conducted a series of massive military exercises.

These are just some of the reasons why our military leaders, including the Chairman of the Joint Chiefs of Staff, have recently testified to this committee that Russia represents the greatest threat to the United—that the United States faces. Whether we agree with that assessment or not, it is a striking wake-up call about the threat Russia poses. And I believe it requires us to think far more seriously about an old mission that our defense establishment has focused less on in recent decades: deterrence.

In response to the challenge that Russia poses in Europe and in the Middle East and in the Arctic, it is not that the United States has done nothing. The problem is, nothing we are doing appears to be deterring Russian aggression. None of us want a return to the Cold War, but we need to face the reality that we are dealing with a Russian ruler who wants exactly that. As such, we must revisit the question what it'll take to deter the conflict and aggression while confronting a revisionist Russia.

We look forward to the thoughts and recommendations from our distinguished witnesses on these questions.

Senator Reed.

STATEMENT OF SENATOR JACK REED

Senator REED. Thank you very much, Mr. Chairman.

Let me first welcome the witnesses, thank them not only for their testimony but for their service to the Nation over so many years and in so many ways.

This morning, our hearing focuses on developments in Russian strategy and military operations which are causing fundamental shifts in the security environment, not only in Europe, but in the Middle East, the Arctic, and elsewhere. The United States and its allies are facing an increasingly aggressive and revanchist Russia and a Putin regime that is willing to use all tools at its disposal, including its military power, to achieve its goals.

Putin's goals appear to be, first, regime survival in the face of Russia's economic, political, and social decline; second, securing Russia's periphery by pressuring its neighbors against integrating with the West; and third, exploiting opportunities to weaken Western unity by dividing member states within the EU and NATO against each other. Yet, Russia's provocative and dangerous aggression often appears opportunistic and potentially harmful for its long-term interests.

Last month, I had the opportunity to visit the Ukraine, where the nascent democratic government in Kyiv is struggling to defend its sovereignty against aggression from Russia and Russian-backed separatists. Russia has demonstrated, in Crimea and in eastern Ukraine, its willingness to use military force to violate Ukraine's territorial integrity and intimidate its neighbor. It is clear that President Putin sees a functioning democratic westward-oriented Ukraine as a threat to his regime's survival domestically and to Russia's broader regional security strategy.

Recently, Russia has shifted its tactics in Ukraine from an emphasis on territorial gains to hybrid warfare and proxy forces to an expansion of his activities aimed at destabilizing the Ukrainian government and economy. This shift in Russian tactics is a result of several factors, including the determination of the Ukrainian forces and people to resist Russian aggression, international sanctions that are proving costly to Russia, the difficulty of disguising casualties from the Russian people, which is engendering some opposition within Russia, and, most recently, a possible desire by President Putin to shift the focus away from Ukraine and toward the conflict in Syria. Russian military operations in the Donbas have been a proving ground for its hybrid warfare technologies, which continue to evolve with increasing sophistication.

The United States needs to be firm in its support of Ukraine, right now, or else the United States and NATO will have a bigger problem in the future. If Ukraine does not weather the current crisis, then Russia's aggressive behavior will be repeated elsewhere, potentially threatening NATO members. The United States needs to act in concert with our allies to assist Ukraine. One immediate need is for the international community to press Russia not to support the illegitimate local elections called by the separatists which violate the specific terms of the Minsk agreement in Ukrainian law. The outcome of the local elections of the Donbas threaten to further undermine the prospects for negotiations as part of the Minsk peace process. I understand that just recently the elections in the conflict area have been postponed until February. The United States and its allies and partners must immediately agree on an approach that supports Ukrainian efforts to hold elections under Ukrainian law, pressures Russia to uphold the terms of the Minsk agreements, and makes clear that any separatist victors in sham elections will not be accepted in participants—as participants in future talks under Minsk.

The United States and its partners should take other steps to counter Russian aggression in Ukraine, as well. Ukraine's need for defensive weapons, including counter-artillery radars and anti-tank weapons, remains critical. Other action to help Ukraine include expanding the training in Ukraine of units of the Ministry of Defense, training Ukrainian forces at facilities outside Ukraine on key defensive weapon systems should a decision to be made to transfer those systems, and exploring options for developing Ukraine's capability to produce domestically much needed weapons, such as anti-tank weapons and vehicles.

In Syria, much as it did in Ukraine, Russia has hidden its true intentions, using the ruse of joining the fight against ISIL to provide a cover for Russia's military intervention to prop up the Assad regime. Russians' actions, however, increasingly expose their true objectives. Instead of focusing on targeting ISIL, Russian airstrikes have predominantly occurred in Homs and Hama, areas controlled by moderate Syrian forces challenging the Assad regime. And yesterday, it was reported that Russian ships in the Caspian Sea launched missiles against a coalition of Syrian opposition forces that does not include ISIL. Russia is providing broader enabling support to the Assad regime's forces against the moderate opposition.

These Russian missile attacks and enabling support were apparently conducted in coordination with a new ground offensive by the Syrian army, Iran's terrorist proxy, Hezbollah, and other Iranian-affiliated forces. This alignment of terrorists and their state sponsors is alarming.

Russia's open military intervention in a conflict well beyond its borders marks a significant departure from how Russia has operated in the past and suggests that President Putin may be attaching particular strategic importance to Russia's access to bases in the overall relationship with Syria. And I hope our witnesses will provide their assessment of the strategic significance of Russia's decision to deploy its military forces to Syria.

Russia's unilateral and belligerent efforts are not helpful to the efforts of the unified coalition of 60-plus countries fighting ISIL and create a dangerous risk of unintended consequences. President Putin has chosen not to join the international anti-ISIL coalition; instead, Putin has chosen to align with Iran and Hezbollah to attack Syria and is seeking to end the brutality of the Assad regime and establish a better Syria. Russians' actions are likely to only prolong and further complicate this conflict. Russia appears to be seeking to keep Bashar Assad in office and maintain Syria as a client state. In addition, Russia, Iran, and Iraq have concluded an intelligence-sharing agreement, and Iraqi Prime Minister Abadi has suggested that Iraq would welcome Russian airstrikes against ISIL in Iraq, adding to the concerns over unintended consequences. Once again, the witnesses' perspective on these issues would be absolutely critical.

Finally, Russia is staking a claim in the Arctic, expanding its military presence, including coastal defense in the north to be able to control movements to a northern passage. Again, this is another area where your comments would be appreciated.

Thank you, Mr. Chairman.

And thank the four witnesses.

Senator MCCAIN. Thank you.

We'll begin with you, General Keane, since you're the oldest one here.

[Laughter.]

STATEMENT OF GENERAL JOHN M. KEANE, USA (RET.), CHAIRMAN, INSTITUTE FOR THE STUDY OF WAR AND FORMER VICE CHIEF OF STAFF OF THE ARMY

General KEANE. Thank you, good morning. Chairman McCain, Ranking Member Reed, distinguished members of the committee. I'm honored to be back testifying before this great committee who means so much to our national defense and security.

It's a privilege to be here with my panel colleagues, particularly General Jones, who I've served with in the Pentagon and have known for years.

Please refer to the maps that you have at your seat, provided by the Institute of War, which I will reference in my remarks.

As to Russian strategy and military operations in Syria, establishing an out-of-region airbase in Syria that is isolated from the heartland of Russia in a war zone is quite unprecedented, particularly for a non-expeditionary military. You can see, on the map labeled ''Russian Deployment to Syria,'' the air-bridges routes over Iran and Iraq, and a sea-bridge route through the Black Sea.

The airbase consists of combat aircraft, helicopters, drones, logistics, support infrastructure, and a battalion-plus of armor infantry, artillery, and air defense for protection of the base. Approximately 2,000 to 3,000 personnel make up the base, which also houses a joint operations center consisting of Russian, Syrian, Iranian, and Hezbollah military personnel, largely now for targeting.

While one can only speculate about the reason for this brazen military aggression, some realities in Syria are insightful. Look at the map labeled ''Control of Terrain in Syria.'' As you can see, the regime control area, in orange, which is now only about 20 percent of Syria. Note the opposition control area to the north and south, in yellow, as the regime is quite confined. Particularly in the north, with the fall of Idlib Province recently, the opposition force is beginning to encroach on the Alawite coastal enclave in Latakia Province, which represents Assad's main political support. Not labeled on the map, in the gray zone, to the east of Homs and Damascus, in central Syria, ISIS seized Palmyra City, the famed ancient city, and a nearby regime airbase, opening up the east-west transportation corridor from Homs to the Iraq border. Syria is Russia's foothold in the Middle East, and, as such, the Tartus Naval Base is a strategic asset. It seems apparent that Russia believed the Assad regime's survival was in a more precarious position and needed to be propped up. As such, if you look at the map labeled ''Russian Airstrikes,'' you can see the focus of the airstrikes are against the opposition forces threatening the regime from the north in Idlib, Hama, and Homs Province. The moderate opposition forces, many trained by the CIA, and Jabhat al-Nusra, an al-Qaeda affiliate, are the main focus with ISIS strikes at Raqqa and near Palmyra are far less significant. Russian cruise missiles were introduced yesterday, striking 11 targets in northern Syria, northwestern Syria, and northeastern Syria. The purpose, then, of the airstrikes are twofold. One is to stop the advance of the opposition forces threatening the regime. And, two, to begin to set conditions for a ground counteroffensive to retake lost territory, with the main effort in the north in southern Idlib and northern Hama Provinces. The Syrian army began limited ground operations yesterday in Idlib Province, obviously supported by Russian airpower. A supporting effort may also be launched to retake Palmyra and the military airbase if the regime can generate sufficient forces.

Even more significant than Russia entering a civil war is their recent strategic alliance with Iran, which will impact every country in the region and further diminish U.S. influence and U.S. interests in the region. Russia has been leveraging this reality to their own advantage by entering into arms deals with Saudi Arabia, UAE, Kuwait, and Egypt. These countries purchasing Russian weapons are not primarily driven by the desire to have Russian equipment, but by the harsh reality of the changing geopolitical landscape, and their desire to have a relationship with Russia has leverage against their strategic enemy: Iran. Russia is also in preliminary discussions to build nuclear powerplants in Saudi Arabia, Jordan, Egypt, and Tunisia. The relationship with Iran and its proxies matters to Russia because it provides them greater influence in the Middle East while also acting as a strategic buffer against radical Islam, a threat which is of great concern to Russia.

Secondly, Russian strategy and military operations in Ukraine and Europe. Putin has put Russia on a path to be a world power with global influence. Most historical world powers have strong economies and strong militaries. Russia—the former Soviet Union was never prosperous, but certainly had a very strong military. Putin was on a path to do just that again with his military when the economy tanked. He was able to modernize his nuclear weapons, but left him with a conventional military that is still no match to the United States and NATO. But, about a third of his military are good units with some select excellent capabilities. This is a land-centric force with good combat aircraft, bombers, and submarines, and a limited power-projection navy with only one aircraft carrier.

Russia's strategy in Europe, I think, is influenced by the Napoleonic and Nazi invasions and the strategic buffer that existed in Europe as part of the Warsaw Pact protecting the heartland of Russia for almost 50 years. These buffer countries are now a part of NATO, which Putin sees as a security risk.

After Putin lost his political stooge, Yanukovych, who he thought would stop the Ukraine movement to the West, he immediately annexed Crimea, correctly believing the Europeans and Americans would be stunned into compliance, thus recovering at home from the embarrassment of Yanukovych's forced departure. Encouraged by their success, Putin moved on eastern Ukraine, introducing hybrid warfare, a combination of special operations forces and intelligence security officers to help create public unrest, then arm and organize that unrest into fighting units, and, when the host country army moves to put the movement down, bring in Russian-disguised conventional military to defeat the army.

Russia's use of military force in Ukraine is very revealing, as it relies heavily on drones to detect Ukrainian military units, with target information relayed immediately to artillery batteries and, within a few minutes, massive artillery is landing on a target, some with thermobaric shells creating a fire incendiary on the unit which is quite devastating. As such, the separatists, supported by Russian military, have consolidated Luhansk and Donetsk Provinces, but denied the land bridge to Mariupol.

The political is more significant, because the Kyiv government has given up on any formal economic or, certainly, military alignment with Europe or NATO. Putin wants the Kyiv to fail and be replaced by a more friendly Russian government. Putin will continue the pressure. And see the map labeled ''Current Proposed Russian Bases'' with the two new permanent ground force bases that are under construction across from the Ukrainian border, the—obviously in Russia—and the airbase Putin has muscled into Belarus which is also now under construction.

So, what are U.S. options? U.S. strategy should be to assure our allies and friends, deter Russian aggression, defeat ISIS, and, long term, as a part of a global alliance, defeat radical Islam. Putin believes that European and American leadership is weak. Putin is counting on the U.S. fear of escalation and fear of confrontation to stop any thought of retaliation. Historically, aggression unanswered has led to more aggression.

As to Syria options, recognize the anti-ISIS strategy in Iraq and Syria is failing. We are certain to lose the war unless there is major and comprehensive change to build an effective and decisive ground force in Syria while removing restrictions on the air campaign to dramatically increase airstrike effectiveness. We need to continue the U.S. policy to force Assad from power, but let's be realistic. Understand that Russia, as Assad's protector, will now play the decisive role. Putin has begun a proxy war with the United States when Russian combat aircraft struck continuously moderate rebel forces trained by the Central Intelligence Agency. This was no accident. Targets were provided by the Syrian regime, and they were accurate. How can the United States stand by and do nothing?

United States military should have been given the mission to retaliate. Options likely to be considered, among many others: crater the al-Assad runway, establish free zones that are, essentially, no-bomb zones as sanctuaries for refugees and U.S.-backed opposition groups, strike Assad's helicopter fleet that is barrel-bombing its own people, just to name a few.

Also, advise Russia that the United States and the coalition will conduct air operations anytime, anywhere in Syria, and the Russians should stay out of our way if they want to avoid confrontation. Unfortunately, United States aircraft are rarely flying now against ISIS targets in Syria, and focusing their efforts in Iraq.

If we continue to wring our hands and continue to be dominated by fears and opposed to instilling fear, then Russian aggression will not just advance in the Middle East, it will, with certainty, escalate in the Baltics and in eastern Europe.

As to Ukraine and Europe's options, recognize further that Russia is not finished in Ukraine, as the new military bases across the border suggest. There is still time to expand the United States military training of Ukraine battalions, which is an effective program, and provide, finally, defensive weapons and capabilities that would definitely make a difference, such as anti-tank missiles, non-missile air defense to counter the drones, counterfire radar to detect the artillery, download intelligence from all source capabilities, et cetera.

The Atlantic Resolve, the name for the U.S.-NATO rotational troop deployments to the Baltics, Poland, Romania, and Hungary, are helpful but a small deterrence to Russian aggression. Russian aggression has already begun in the Baltics—that is, it's pounding the Russian-speaking minorities in the Baltics with continuous propaganda to create unrest and to foment a split with the nation's majority, coupled with continuous airspace violations that obviously are harassing the host governments.

Department of Defense must reevaluate its stationing plan for the combatant commands, in view of a revisionist and aggressive

Russia. The Pacific is the largest combatant command, with over 400,000 troops, while Europe is considerably smaller and less than adequate, now down to around 50,000. The assumptions that drove the downsizing of the United States military positions in Europe have obviously changed, and we need a relook.

In conclusion, Russia is clearly challenging U.S. influence and interests in the Middle East as the dominant outside regional country while also seeking to challenge NATO in eastern Europe and possibly NATO's very existence. Our allies in both regions must be convinced that the United States stand behind them. Now is the time for a firm hand, but the United States should not close off communications with Russia and continue to pursue opportunities where there is mutual interest.

Thank you, Mr. Chairman. And I look forward to your questions.

[The prepared statement of General Keane follows:]

PREPARED STATEMENT BY GENERAL JOHN M. KEANE

Chairman McCain, ranking member Reed, distinguished members of the committee, am honored to be back testifying today on Russia and the crisis in Syria and the Ukraine. It's a privilege to be here with my panel colleagues, particularly General Jones, who I served with in the Pentagon and have known for years. Please refer to the maps provided by the Institute for the Study of War (ISW) which I will reference in my remarks.

1. RUSSIAN STRATEGY AND MILITARY OPERATIONS IN SYRIA:

Russia began air strikes in Syria about a week ago after rapidly establishing a forward operating air base at Al Assad airfield in Latakia province, some 36 miles north of their Naval base at Tartous. Establishing an out of region air base, that is isolated from the heartland of Russia, in a war zone, is quite unprecedented, particularly for a non expeditionary military.

To establish and sustain this airbase you can see on the map labeled 'Russian Deployment to Syria', the air bridge routes over Iran and Iraq and the sea bridge route through the Black Sea taking approximately 4 days to transit. The air base consists of combat aircraft, helicopters, drones, logistics support infrastructure, and a battalion plus of armor, infantry, artillery and air defense for protection of the base. Approximately 2K to 3K personnel make up the base which also houses a joint operations center consisting of Russian, Syrian, Iranian and Hezbollah military personnel.

While one can only speculate about the reason for this brazen military aggression some realities in Syria are insightful. After 4 years of civil war the Syrian military, numbers about 125K down from a high of 220K. The Army is beset with low morale, desertion and equipment problems with the Air Force losing about 1 to 2 aircraft per month due to combat or accident. During the last year the opposition force has gained steadily on the regime forces with some gains operationally significant.

Please look at the map labeled 'Control of Terrain in Syria' and you can see the regime control area in orange which is now only about 20% of Syria. Note the opposition control area to the north and south of the orange as the regime is quite confined. Particularly in the north with the fall of Idlib province recently, the opposition force is beginning to encroach on the Alawite coastal enclave in Latakia province which represents Assad's main political support. In the last several months there has been some erosion of this Alawite support. To the east of Homs and Damascus in central Syria ISIS seized Palmyra city and a nearby regime airbase opening up the east-west transportation corridor from Homs to the Iraq border. We at ISW suspect that the Iranians who are in Syria in far greater number than the Russians (7K to 100 plus) and have very good situational awareness, raised the alarm to the Russians during multiple visits to Moscow by Iranian Revolutionary Guard Corps (IRGC) leaders to include a much reported visit by Qasem Soleimani.

Russia has a 60 plus year relationship with Syria dating back to post WWII as the former Soviet Union. Syria is Russia's foothold in the Middle East (M.E.) and as such the Tartous Naval base is a strategic asset that is much valued. It seems apparent that Russia believed the Assad regime survival was in a more precarious position and needed to be propped up. As such if you look at the map labeled 'Russian Airstrikes in Syria', you can see the focus of the airstrikes are against the opposition forces threatening the regime from the north in Idlib, Hama and Homs province. The moderate opposition forces, many trained by the CIA and Jabhat al-Nusra, an AQ affiliate, are the main focus with the ISIS targets at Raqqah and near Palmyra are far less significant and likely mere 'window dressing' for the exaggerated narrative that ISIS is the major reason for the Russian presence. Russian cruise missiles were introduced yesterday striking 11 targets in western and eastern Syria.

The purpose then of the airstrikes are twofold: one to stop the advance of the opposition forces threatening the regime and two to begin to set conditions for a ground counter-offensive to retake lost territory with the main effort in the north in southern Idlib province and northern Hama province. Syrian Army limited ground shaping operations began in Idlib province yesterday supported by Russian air. A supporting effort may be launched to retake Palmyra and the military airbase if the regime can generate sufficient forces. Recapturing the ancient city would be a PR victory for Syria and Russia. The counter offensive would likely be jointly planned by Syria and Iranian generals and consist of the Army, the National Defense Force, which are local militias, some actually led and most advised by the IRGC, and the Hezbollah and Iraqi Shia militia. Of course Russia and Syria air power will play a large role in supporting the ground offensive.

Even more significant than Russia entering the Syria civil war is their recent strategic alliance with Iran which will impact every country in the region and further diminish U.S. influence and U.S. interests in the region.

Russia certainly recognizes that the M.E. is experiencing one of the most tumultuous periods in its history with the old order challenged by the aspirational goals of the Arab Spring, Islamic terrorists taking advantage of the political and social upheaval and Iran using proxies to gain influence in Lebanon, Syria, Iraq and Yemen. Furthermore, Russia observed, probably somewhat in disbelief, as the U.S. abandoned Mubarak in Egypt, abandoned Iraq and retreated from Yemen and Libya as part of an unstated policy to disengage from the M.E. to avoid the strategic mistake of another M.E. protracted war. For a year now, Russia has been leveraging this reality to their own advantage by entering into arms deals with Saudi Arabia, UAE, Kuwait and Egypt. Also, there are Russian counter terrorism experts advising the Egyptian military in their fight against ISIS. A country the U.S. had a mil to mil relationship with for 35 years. These countries purchasing Russian weapons who normally buy U.S. and European weapons are not driven by the desire to have Russian equipment but by the harsh reality of the changing geopolitical landscape and their desire to have a relationship with Russia as leverage against their strategic enemy, Iran. Iraq is also purchasing Russian weapons as the promised U.S. flow of weapons has been slow to nonexistent at times and have recently welcomed Russian generals and their staff to join their coordination center in Baghdad to share intelligence with the Iraq Army, the IRGC and the Iraq Shia militia. Russia is also in preliminary discussion to build nuclear power plants in Saudi Arabia, Jordan, Egypt and Tunisia, with all their inherent problems of corruption, fraud, criminality to say nothing of the major security challenge of nuclear power plants. The relationship with Iran and its proxies matters to Russia because it provides them greater influence in the M.E. while also acting as a strategic buffer to their south against radical Islam, a threat which is of great concern to them now in southern Russia.

2. RUSSIAN STRATEGY AND MILITARY OPERATIONS IN UKRAINE/EUROPE:

Vladimir Putin came to power after the economic, political and social chaos of the 1990's following the collapse of the Soviet Union and ending the decade with their own military in shambles and suffering the public humiliation of his Serbian ally, Milosevic, not only losing all 4 wars he fought but being bombed into oblivion by the Americans in a 78 day air campaign.

Putin certainly shaped, in part, by these events and his life as a KGB officer tightens internal security and control, crushes the Chechens, represses political opposition, takes control of the media, and puts Russia on a path to be a world power with global influence. Most historical world powers have strong economies and strong militaries, Russia, the former Soviet Union was never prosperous but certainly had a strong military. Putin was on a path to do just that again with his military when the economy tanked, leaving him with a military that is no match to the U.S. and NATO but with about 1/3rd good units with some select excellent capabilities. This is a land centric force with good combat aircraft, bombers, submarines, and a limited power projection Navy with only one aircraft carrier.

Russia's strategy in Europe is influenced by the Napoleonic and Nazi invasions and the strategic buffer that existed in eastern Europe as part of the Warsaw Pact, protecting the heartland of Russia for almost 50 years. These buffer countries are now a part of NATO, which Putin sees as a security risk.

As such Putin saw Ukraine, which is a food breadbasket for Russia, being threatened by the desire of many Ukrainians to politically, economically and militarily align with the European Union and potentially NATO. After Putin lost his political stooge, Yanukovych who he thought would stop the Ukraine movement to the West, he immediately annexed Crimea, correctly believing the Europeans and Americans would be stunned into compliance, thus recovering at home from the embarrassment of Yanukovych's departure. Encouraged by success, Putin moved on eastern Ukraine introducing hybrid warfare, a combination of SOF and intell officers to help create popular unrest, organize sympathizers into fighting units and when the host country Army moves to put down the movement, bring in Russian disguised conventional military to defeat the Army.

Russia's use of military force in Ukraine is very revealing as it relies heavily on drones to detect Ukrainian military units with target information relayed to artillery batteries and within a few minutes, massive artillery is landing on the target, some with thermobaric shells creating a fire incendiary on the unit, which is quite devastating. As such, the separatists supported by Russian military have consolidated Luhansk and Donetsk provinces but denied the land bridge to Mariupol.

The political result is more significant because the Kiev government has given up on any economic or certainly military alignment with Europe or NATO. Putin wants the Kiev government to fail and be replaced by a more friendly Russian government. Putin will continue the pressure, see the map labeled 'Current/Proposed Russian Bases Near Ukraine,' with the two new permanent ground force bases that are under construction across from the Ukrainian border in Russia and the air base Putin is building in Belarus.

3. U.S. OPTIONS

• Overall:

U.S. strategy should be to *assure* our allies and friends, *deter* Russian aggression and *defeat* ISIS initially and, long term, as a part of a global alliance to *defeat* radical Islam. Putin believes that European and American leadership is weak and has consistently out-maneuvered and out bluffed the U.S. and its allies. Putin is counting on the U.S. fear of escalation and fear of confrontation to stop any thought of retaliation. Aggression unanswered, historically, has led to more aggression.

• Syria Options:

- Recognize the anti ISIS strategy in Iraq and Syria is failing and we are certain to lose the war unless there is major and comprehensive change to build an effective and decisive ground force in Syria and Iraq while removing restrictions on the air campaign to dramatically increase airstrike capability. Continue U.S. policy to force Assad from power, but understand that Russia, as Assad's protector will now play a decisive role.

- Deter: Putin has begun a proxy war with the U.S. when Russian combat aircraft struck, continuously, moderate rebel forces trained by the CIA. This was no accident, targets were provided by the Syrian regime and they were accurate. How can the U.S. stand by and do nothing? U.S. military should have been given the mission to retaliate. Options likely to be considered among others: crater the Al Assad runway, establish free zones that are sanctuaries for refugees, strike Assad's helicopter fleet that is barrel bombing, just to name a few.

- Deter: Advise Russia that the U.S. and the coalition will conduct air operations anytime, anywhere in Syria and that they should stay out of our way if they want to avoid confrontation. Believe U.S. aircraft are rarely flying now against ISIS targets in Syria.

- If we continue to wring our hands and continue to be dominated by fear and opposed to instilling fear, the Russian aggression will not just advance in the M.E. but most likely it will escalate in the Baltics and eastern Europe.

• Ukraine / Europe Options:

- Deter: Recognize further that Russia is not finished in Ukraine as the new military bases across the border suggest. There is still time in addition to the U.S. military, training Ukraine battalions, which is an effective program and providing non-lethal aid, to provide defensive weapons and capabilities that would definitely make a difference. Such as: anti tank missiles, non-missile air defense to counter the drones, counter fire radar to detect the artillery, downloaded intelligence from U.S. all source capabilities etc

- Deter: The Atlantic Resolve U.S./NATO rotational troop deployments to the Baltics, Poland, Romania and Hungary are a helpful but a small deterrence to Russian aggression. Russia is pounding the Russian speaking minorities in the Baltics with continuous propaganda to create unrest and to foment a split with the nation's majority. Department of Defense must re-evaluate its stationing plan for the Combatant Commands in view of a revisionist and aggressive Russia. The Pacific is the largest Combatant Command with over 400K troops while Europe is considerably smaller and less than adequate with about 50K. (The Cold War stationing in Europe was approximately 600K).

Larger force commitments permit larger unit rotational deployments and a permanent base structure in the Baltics and eastern Europe. All deployed forces assigned to bases in central Europe no longer makes sense. Obviously, NATO must adjust its priorities as well as the U.S.

In conclusion, Russia is clearly challenging U.S. influence and interest in the M.E. as the dominant outside regional country while also seeking to challenge NATO in eastern Europe and possibly its very existence. While at times this demands a firm hand the U.S. should not close off communications with Russia but continue to pursue opportunities when there is mutual self interest. Such an interest is radical Islam. Russia was and is consumed with radical Islam and its threat which is the primary reason for the war in Afghanistan and prior to 9/11 it fought two major battles with the Chechens. The U.S. and Russia could partner on this issue as both countries have the most experience and could help organize together a global alliance. Another area is partnering on nuclear power plant development and security in the M.E. to the economic benefit of the M.E. while controlling uranium enrichment and plant security. Clearly Russia and the U.S. are in a renewed strategic competitive relationship which still has opportunities for positive engagement for mutual benefit.

Thank you and I look forward to your questions.

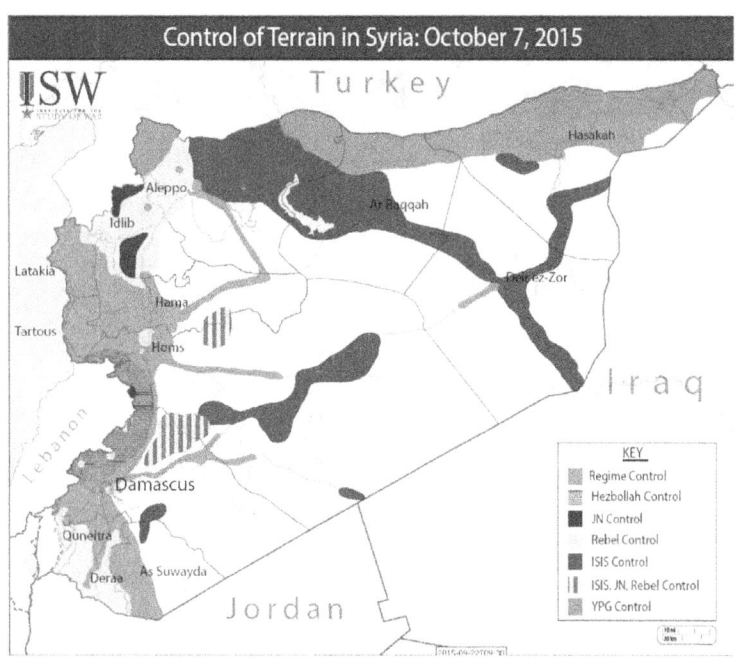

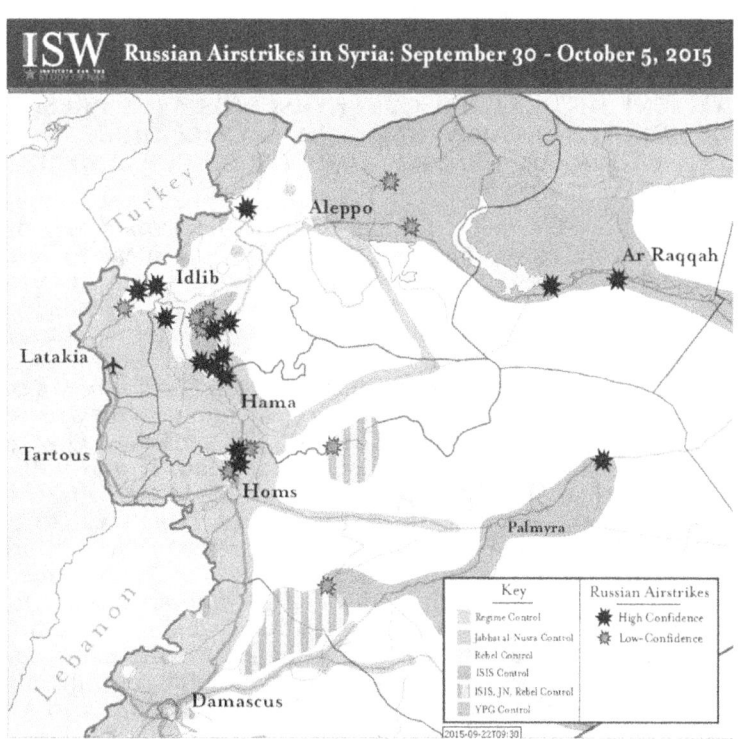

Senator MCCAIN. Thank you.
Ms. Conley.

STATEMENT OF HEATHER CONLEY, SENIOR VICE PRESIDENT FOR EUROPE, EURASIA, AND THE ARCTIC; DIRECTOR, EUROPE PROGRAM, CENTER FOR STRATEGIC AND INTERNATIONAL STUDIES

Ms. CONLEY. Chairman McCain, Senator Reed, members of the committee, thank you so much. It is a privilege to speak to you this morning, as well as join with my fellow panelists to discuss the evolving nature of Russia's growing military threat, which geographically stretches from the Kola Peninsula in the Arctic to the Mediterranean coast of Syria.

In my view, the Kremlin is reconstructing a 21st century version of the Iron Curtain. As General Keane mentioned, they're recreating a strategic buffer which is designed to achieve a new grand international bargain with the West, a Yalta 2.0, if you will, that assures a Russian sphere of influence in Europe and the Middle East. This curtain, like its 20th century predecessor, seeks to block the perceived contagion of democracy and reform while returning Russia to internationally recognized great-power status. This curtain is designed to do several things: deny military access to the West through the construction of new, and the revitalization of former, Russian military bases. It is designed to ensure the continuous exercising of air, land, and sea capabilities at full combat readiness. It rapidly mobilizes substantial Russian forces in a very short period of time. It's designed to deploy a variety of hybrid economic and political tactics which are at its disposal. And, finally, it employs an extremely effective counter-factual strategic communications campaign.

Now, this 21st century curtain also has a built-in Kremlin-controlled thermostat. President Putin can turn up the heat when and where he wants, as he's done in eastern Ukraine; and when it is needed, he can turn down the heat, as we're seeing right now. And then he can shift to a different portion of this curtain, as he is doing in Syria. The West will continue to react to the Kremlin's actions rather than proactively shape and deter them.

Russia's military modernization in the Arctic is the perfect example of how this new curtain, or, as I suggest in a new CSIS report, an ''ice curtain,'' has been constructed. Russia has held three major military exercises in the Arctic over the last 24 months. The first exercise was part of a larger Zapad 2013 military exercise, which focused on Russia's western military district, and it demonstrated a more streamlined command structure, more efficient tactical units, and the ability to deploy a large-scale complex military operation coordinated with other areas of operation. This exercise fully demonstrated that Russia has a much larger spatial definition of its theater of operations, which extends from the Arctic to the Black Sea.

The second exercise, in September of 2014, was the largest post-Soviet military exercises that we have seen. It was held in the Russian far east, and it was preceded by a snap military exercise. Vostok 2014 involved over 100,000 servicemen and demonstrated a complex display of air, maritime, and land components. And this exercise was partly conducted on new military bases in the Russian Arctic, New Siberian Islands, and Wrangel Island, which some believe simulated an exercise to repel U.S. and NATO forces.

And then, finally, in March of this year we saw the third and most culminating exercise, which was a snap military exercise in the Arctic which consisted of 45,000 Russian forces, 15 submarines, and 41 warships at full combat readiness. We did not know that they were going to do this.

So, this extraordinary exercise tempo, the threefold increase in Russian air incursions over the Arctic, Baltic, and North Seas over the past 12 months, as well as Russia's announcement that will—it will have a total of 14 operational airfields in the Russian Arctic by the end of this year, 50 airfields by 2020, and a 30-percent increase in Russian special forces deployed to the Arctic, all underscore that the Arctic is becoming a major theater of operations for Russia. The Arctic region has now been included in Russia's amended military doctrine, as of December of last year, and in its new maritime doctrine, which was just released in July. And it is under a new command, the Russian Northern Fleet United Strategic Command for the Arctic.

Now, the conclusions that we draw from Russia's military behavior is that it is increasingly able to project significant anti-access, anti-denial capabilities in the Arctic, the north Atlantic, and, increasingly, the north Pacific, which demonstrates the ability to rapidly deploy both conventional and unconventional forces. What is perhaps the most disturbing has been Russia's focus on enhancing its nuclear deterrent in the Arctic, where it has simulated massive retaliatory attacks in the Barents Sea. Our Norwegian and British allies—and I know, Senator McCain, you were recently in the region—have witnessed a surge in Russian submarine activity in the north Atlantic.

So, let me just very briefly describe the remaining geographic contours of this 21st century curtain. The curtain proceeds from the Arctic, south to the Finnish-Russian border. Russia has returned to an abandoned military base 50 kilometers from the Finnish border, where the 1st Russian Infantry Brigade has arrived with 3,000 soldiers anticipated. The curtain proceeds to the Russian exclave of Kaliningrad, home of the Russian Baltic Fleet, where vessels from the fleet have delivered fighter jets and Asconder missile launchers capable of launching both conventional and nuclear missiles. Russia has recently installed new S–400 missile batteries and has increased its force presence.

The curtain then transitions from ice to steel on the Polish-Belarusian border, where President Putin has just ordered Russian officials to construct, with its Belarusian counterparts, a new military base in Belarus. This is the first time a newly constructed military base will be outside of Russia since the collapse of the Soviet Union. This base will station SU–27 fighters.

The curtain, of course, extends fully to Ukraine, where Russia has an estimated 29,000 soldiers in occupied Crimea, a substantially increased Baltic Sea fleet, which it plans to augment with 30 additional vessels by 2020.

The curtain then continues, going, of course, as General Keane explained, through eastern Ukraine and extremely capable forces on the Russian-Ukrainian border, in fact, commencing construction of new installations that will potentially contain significant munitions ordnance facilities.

Ukraine, of course, we move to Transnistria and Moldova, where there are 1500 troops—Russian troops stationed as peacekeepers. And, of course, from Russia's invasion of Georgia in 2008, we have Russian military presence in South Ossetia and Abkhazia. And, in fact, the Russians have been pushing out this territory. They are 100 kilometers from the main Georgian highway that would divide Georgia. So, they're increasing their territorial gains. And, as we've seen extensive—this curtain continues, then, to Armenia, where Russia is further augmenting its forces, and then, as we know, from—to Syria.

So, how can the U.S. and NATO respond to this new curtain of ice and steel? I'd like to commend the committee. The National Defense Authorization Act is a really great point of departure. And I commend the bipartisan resolve to seek to assess these challenges and identify critical gaps. For far too long, we've discounted Russia's military capabilities and did not take their threats and pronouncements seriously. We can no longer afford that luxury.

But, simply assessing the problem is woefully insufficient. Painful budget and force-posture decisions must now be taken. We cannot reset this challenge away, and we cannot get back to business as usual. The West has forgotten how to conduct effective deterrence in the Modern Age against a sophisticated adversary. Deterrence is as effective as the credibility on which it stands.

The United States immediately and positively responded to requests for U.S. forces to be sent to the Baltic states, Poland, and Romania, when requested last spring without pondering the decision for months. The strong bipartisan support for the European Reassurance Initiative was another important signal of U.S. resolve. This act strengthened U.S. and NATO's Article 5 credibility, but these actions were viewed as temporary measures to change President Putin's behavior in Ukraine. This has not achieved its objectives, and now we need a more durable deterrence posture.

U.S. and North Atlantic Treaty Organization (NATO) forces, accompanied by significant air and maritime components, must increase their presence on NATO's northern and eastern flanks. The U.S. should seriously consider sending a third combat brigade to Europe to reinforce both flanks while strongly encouraging our European allies to increase their force presence, as well.

NATO must initiate the pre-positioning of military equipment in the region, not simply for exercise purposes only, and immediately address identified shortcomings in secure communications and infrastructure needs that were identified during Operation Atlantic Resolve this year, as well as continue to increase the number of regional exercise. We must ensure rapid deployability. And that is where we are lacking.

It is time, to echo General Keane's comments, for a comprehensive review of U.S. force posture in Europe for the next 5 to 10 years. It is for this reason that the outcome of next year's NATO summit in Warsaw is absolutely critical. If NATO simply decides to review the decisions it reached at its last summit, the alliance will have failed to address its most significant security challenge since the end of the Cold War. The summit must launch a long-term strategic adaptation to what will be a long-term and highly destabilizing challenge.

Mr. Chairman, on one final note and a word of caution, as much as the U.S. and NATO must do more to deter future Russian military aggression, we must also be fully cognizant of the devastating impact of Russian influence inside NATO that inhibit allies from taking collective action against Russia. As Russia dominates the media, financial, and energy markets of some of our NATO allies, we will find NATO collectively less able to respond. This requires as much policy attention by the U.S. and NATO as it does to militarily deter the Kremlin.

I thank you, Mr. Chairman.

[The prepared statement of Ms. Conley follows:]

CSIS | CENTER FOR STRATEGIC &
INTERNATIONAL STUDIES

Statement before the

Senate Armed Services Committee

"RUSSIAN STRATEGY AND MILITARY OPERATIONS"

A Testimony by:

Heather Conley

Senior Vice President for Europe, Eurasia, and the Arctic

Director, Europe Program

Center for Strategic and International Studies (CSIS)

October 8, 2015

126 Hart Senate Office Building

WWW.CSIS.ORG   1616 RHODE ISLAND AVENUE NW   TEL. (202) 887.0200
WASHINGTON, DC 20036   FAX (202) 775.3199

Chairman McCain, Ranking Member Reed, Members of the Committee, it is a privilege to speak to you this morning as well as join with my fellow panelists to discuss the evolving nature of Russia's growing military threat which geographically stretches from the Kola Peninsula in the Arctic to the Mediterranean coast of Syria.

Russia is back as a geopolitically destabilizing state actor. After experiencing a period of relative peace and security in Europe over the past 25 years – and with the exception of the brutality of the conflicts in Bosnia and Kosovo in the 1990s – the transatlantic community believed that these twenty-five years were the new, post-modern norm. Unfortunately, I believe we will come to view this post-Cold War period as an exceptional moment of security that has now passed. We have returned to balance of power politics where Russia – with increasing frequency – uses military means to achieve its political objectives. The transatlantic community's response to Russia's invasion of its neighbors – and indeed its first talking point – is to take the military option immediately off the table. The West then seeks to establish a diplomatic course guaranteed to ensure the intractability of the very problem that Russia has created, eventually hoping to "reset" its troubled relationship and achieve agreements on broader strategic issues.

The Kremlin is reconstructing a 21st Century version of the Iron Curtain which is designed to achieve a new grand international bargain with the West – Yalta 2.0 if you will – that assures a Russian sphere of influence in Europe and the Middle East. This curtain, like its 20th century predecessor, seeks to block the perceived contagion of democracy and reform while returning Russia to internationally recognized great power status. This curtain denies military access to the West through the construction of new and a revitalization of former Russian military bases; ensures the continuous exercising of air, land and sea capabilities at full combat readiness; rapidly mobilizes substantial Russian forces in a short period of time; deploys a variety of hybrid economic and political tactics which are at its disposal; and employs an effective counterfactual strategic communications campaign.

This 21st century curtain also has a built-in, Kremlin-controlled thermostat: President Putin can turn up the heat as he has done in eastern Ukraine, and, when it is needed, he can turn down the heat and shift to a different portion of the curtain as he is now doing in Syria. The West will continue to react to the Kremlin's actions rather than pro-actively shape and deter them.

Russia's military modernization in the Arctic is a perfect example of how this new curtain or, as I suggest in a new CSIS report – an ice curtain – has being formed. Russia has held three major military exercises in the Arctic over the past 24 months. The first instance was a simultaneous exercise around the Kola Peninsula which was part of the larger, Zapad 2013 military exercise, which demonstrated a more streamlined command structure, more efficient tactical units and the ability to deploy a large scale, complex military operation that is coordinated with other areas of operation. This exercise demonstrated that Russia has a larger spatial definition of its theatre of operations, extending from the Arctic to the Black Sea.

The second exercise, in September 2014, was the largest post-Soviet military exercise and was held in the Russian Far East. Preceded by a snap military exercise, Vostok-2014 involved over 100,000 servicemen and a complex display of air, maritime and land components. This exercise was partly conducted on a new military base in the Russian Arctic New Siberian Islands and Wrangel Island which some analysts believe simulated Russian forces repelling a U.S. or NATO invasion. This exercise focused on rapid mobilization, combined operations and demonstrated use of both conventional and unconventional forces. The third and culminating exercise occurred in March 2015 when President Putin announced a snap military exercise that consisted of 45,000 Russian forces, 15 submarines and 41 warships at full combat readiness in the Arctic. This extraordinary exercise tempo, the three-fold increase in Russian air incursions over the Arctic, Baltic and North Seas over the past twelve months and Russia's announcement that it will have a total of 14 operational airfields in the Russian Arctic by the end of this year, 50 airfields by 2020 and a 30 percent increase of Russian Special forces in the Arctic suggests that the Arctic has emerged as a major theatre of operations for Russia. Defending against future military threats, the Arctic region has now been included in Russia's amended military (December 2014) and maritime (July 2015) doctrines and will be coordinated by a new Russian Northern Fleet-United Strategic Command for the Arctic.

The conclusions that we draw from Russia's military behavior in the Arctic over the past 24 months are that Russia is increasingly able to project significant anti-access/anti-denial capabilities in the Arctic, the North Atlantic and increasingly in the North Pacific while demonstrating the ability to rapidly deploy both conventional and nonconventional forces throughout the theatre. What is perhaps most disturbing has been Russia's focus on enhancing its nuclear deterrent in the Arctic which it has simulated massive retaliatory attacks in the Barents Sea. Our Norwegian and British allies have also witnessed a surge in Russian submarine activity in the North Atlantic.

From the Arctic, Russia's military presence increases along the new ice curtain south to the Finnish – Russian border. Russia has returned to its abandoned military base 50 kilometers from the Finnish border where the first Russian infantry brigade has arrived with 3,000 soldiers anticipated at the base. The curtain proceeds to the Russian exclave of Kaliningrad, home of the Russian Baltic Fleet, where vessels from the fleet have delivered fighter jets and Iskander missile launchers capable of launching both conventional and nuclear missiles. Russia has recently installed new S-400 missile batteries and increased its force presence. The arming of Kaliningrad is part of a 19 trillion ruble plan to increase the share of modern weapons in the Russian armed forces' arsenal from 10% to 70%.

The curtain transitions from ice to steel on the Belarussian-Polish border where, despite recent protests and opposition from Belarusian president Alexander Lukashenko, President Putin has ordered Russian officials to work with their Belarusian counterparts to construct a military base in Belarus. Russia already has functional radars and a navy communications facility in Belarus, as well as a number of fighter jets, but this would be the first military base constructed since the end of the Soviet Union. It would be used to station SU-27 fighters.

The curtain has been fully constructed in Ukraine where, in March, Russia had an estimated 29,000 soldiers in occupied Crimea and has substantially increased its Black Sea Fleet, adding a new base in the city of Novorossiysk and plans 30 additional vessels by 2020. The curtain extends through eastern Ukraine where it is estimated that there are currently 12,000 Russian troops stationed and where the pro-Russian separatists have fully integrated in the Russian command structure. Russia has also commenced construction of a new installation on the Russian-Ukrainian border near the town of Soloti, which is expected to contain munitions and ordnance depots, training facilities, as well as barracks capable of housing several thousand troops.

From Ukraine, the curtain extends through Transnistria where the Kremlin has roughly 1,500 troops stationed as "peacekeepers." Following the 2008 Russian invasion of Georgia, Russia has considerably strengthened its military presence and extended its territorial gains, via South Ossetia and Abkhazia, coming within 100 kilometers of the main highway which divides Georgia. The curtain then extends to the rest of the Caucasus through Armenia where Russia has reinforced its position with nearly 5,000 troops, S-300 missile batteries, tanks, and a fleet of fighter jets and attack helicopters. And, in real time, we are currently witnessing the Russian military build-up in Syria and the first use of Russian cruise missiles in combat.

How can the U.S. and NATO respond to this new curtain of ice and steel?

The National Defense Authorization Act is a very good point of departure and I wish to commend the Committee's bipartisan resolve to seek to assess this challenge and identify capabilities gaps. For too long we discounted Russia's military capabilities and did not take their pronouncements and threats seriously. We can no longer afford this luxury. But simply assessing the problem is woefully insufficient. Painful budget and force posture decisions must now be taken. We cannot "reset" this challenge and we cannot get back to business as usual.

The West has forgotten how to conduct effective deterrence in the modern age against a sophisticated adversary. Deterrence is as effective as the credibility on which it stands. American credibility to militarily deter Russia is at an all-time low. U.S. redlines no longer have meaning following the use of chemical weapons by the Assad regime and the constant diminishment of our negotiating position over Iran's nuclear program. Moreover, the U.S did not support Ukraine by providing it lethal military assistance to defend itself despite the fact that the U.S. provided Ukraine with written bilateral security guarantees.

The United States did, however, immediately and positively respond to requests for U.S. forces from the Baltic States, Poland, and Romania when requested last spring without pondering the decision for months. This act strengthened U.S. and NATO's Article 5 credibility. Yet these actions were viewed as temporary measures to change President Putin's behavior in Ukraine. This temporary posture has not achieved its objectives and therefore a new and more durable deterrence posture is required.

The U.S., along with our NATO allies, will continue to gain credibility by stating clearly and without hyperbole what we intend to do and then do it immediately. When NATO talks tough about Russia's actions in Northern Europe but halves its air policing presence in the Baltic region, we undermine our own credibility. When we announce that NATO will deploy 5,000 soldiers in 48 hours, we do it; we do not explain why airlift is in short supply and why adequate forces cannot be generated.

U.S. leadership – in NATO and bilaterally – must create a long-term and durable response to Russia's new ice and steel curtain. U.S. and NATO forces, accompanied by significant air and maritime components, must increase their presence on NATO's northern and eastern flanks. The U.S. should seriously consider sending a third combat brigade to Europe to reinforce both flanks while engaging European allies to increase their force presence as well. NATO must initiate the prepositioning of military equipment in the region (not simply for exercise purposes), and immediately address shortcomings in secure communications and infrastructure needs as well increase the number of regional exercises to ensure the ability to rapidly deploy. It is time for a comprehensive review of the U.S. force posture in Europe for the next five to ten years.

It is for these reasons that the outcome of next year's NATO Warsaw Summit is so critical. If NATO simply decides to review the decisions of its last summit, the Alliance will have failed to address its most significant security challenge since the end of the Cold War. It is no accident that President Putin has turned down the temperature on the conflict in eastern Ukraine as he turns it up in Syria. In addition to demonstrating that there will be no further international regime change on Putin's watch and to prove to President Obama that Russia is not a regional but a global power, Russia's military involvement in Syria (and the resulting flood of refugees and migrants fleeing to Europe) continues to fuel divisions within NATO that the threat from the "south" – fully aided and abetted by Russia – is greater than the threat from the East for which Russia is fully responsible.

Finally, as much as the U.S. and NATO must do more to deter future Russian military aggression, we must also be fully cognizant of the devastating impact of Russian influence *inside* NATO countries that could inhibit allies from taking collective action against Russia. As Russia dominates the media, financial and energy markets of some of our NATO partners, we will find NATO collectively less able to respond. This requires as much attention by the U.S. and NATO as does militarily deterring the Kremlin.

President Putin gave a speech to the Valdai International Discussion Club last fall entitled, "The World Order: New Rules or a Game without Rules?" The Kremlin rejects the international rules and of the post-World War II order, rules regarding territorial integrity and transparency that Putin's Soviet predecessors accepted. The question is will the U.S. and its allies accept Putin's new rules and new curtain so President Putin can achieve his grand bargain, or is the West willing to challenge and fully reject this construct, like it did during the Cold War era. NATO was born in 1949 as a response to the building of an Iron Curtain; it is up to this generation of leaders to decide how they will respond to a new curtain of ice and steel.

Senator MCCAIN. Ambassador Sestanovich, welcome.

STATEMENT OF HON. STEPHEN SESTANOVICH, GEORGE F. KENNAN SENIOR FELLOW FOR RUSSIAN AND EURASIAN STUDIES, COUNCIL ON FOREIGN RELATIONS, COLUMBIA UNIVERSITY

Ambassador SESTANOVICH. Chairman McCain, Senator Reed, members of the committee, thank you for the opportunity to join your discussion today.

Let me organize just some brief introductory remarks by picking up on two comments on Russia by General Dunford, the new distinguished Chairman of the Joint Chiefs, who, in his confirmation testimony to you this summer, described Russian behavior as ''alarming.'' I completely agree with this. I also disagree with the other thing he said, which was that Russia is an existential threat to the United States. And let me explain why I disagree.

First, when we talk about an existential threat, we mislead ourselves. No matter how alarmed we are by Russia's current behavior, we use the term ''existential threat'' only because of its large strategic nuclear arsenal. And that's a potential threat whether Russia's relations with us are good or bad, or whether Russia's behavior is reckless or wise. Russia has acted recklessly of late, but that has not really increased the existential threat General Dunford spoke of.

Second, this language misleads Russians. It feeds a public mood in Russia that honestly borders on national hysteria. These days, Russian officials routinely say things about the United States that are bizarre and incomprehensible. Unfortunately, hearing that we see Russia as an existential threat—pretty extreme language, after all—tells many Russians that our countries are on a collision course toward war, and that we have accepted that idea. I urge the members of this committee to take a different approach, to challenge responsible Russians to see how strange and counterproductive their country's policies looks to the outside world, not to make ourselves look equally strange.

Now, I said I agree that Russian behavior is alarming. It's really alarming. And we need to appreciate that—not only that it is alarming, but that it doesn't come out of nowhere. This is not something that has just happened in the past year or two.

First—a few quick points on this—Russian actions in the Middle East and in Ukraine reflect the doubling and more of their defense budget in the past 10 years 50-percent increase just since the end of the financial crisis, in the past 5 years. This program of modernization is still unfolding, and the biggest procurement projects are ahead. As Russia's capabilities have increased, so has its anti-Western rhetoric. The official military doctrine of Russia identifies both NATO and the United States as threats to Russia.

Secondly, Russian actions reflect the new nationalism of Russian public opinion. The seizure of Crimea and continuing attempts to fragment eastern Ukraine have given this nationalist mood an angrier, more embattled tone. Russian decisionmakers feel they can count on public support for more assertive displays of national power. They have to worry, of course, about casualties. And I think we should assume that they are just as worried, and maybe more worried, about casualties in Syria than they have been in Ukraine. But, so far, that concern has not restrained their conduct. Putin's popularity is largely intact.

Third, Russian actions are a response, as President Obama and as General Keane has noted, to the weakness of the Assad regime in Syria, Russia's oldest and now only real ally in the region. President Putin has made clear, as he has in Ukraine, that he is prepared to make a significant military commitment to save embattled clients, no matter how shaky and illegitimate their position is. And he acts this way, in part, because circumstances allow it. In Syria, several years of policy confusion by the United States and Europe have encouraged him. Had the United States imposed a no-fly zone in Syria 3 years ago, there would be no Russian intervention today.

Fourth, Secretary Carter may well be right that Russian policy is doomed to fail. I'm—I think this is entirely possible. But, in the course of failing, it may do a great deal of damage, both in Syria and beyond. It should, therefore, be a goal of the United States and its allies to limit and eventually reverse Russia's intervention. Continued confusion, merely calling on Russia to join the coalition against ISIS, will not achieve this end.

Fifth, anyone responsible for the national security of the United States, like the members of this committee, should worry about where Russia's reckless behavior will lead next. There are many areas in which one could expect troublemaking. We should not, by any means, conclude that we face an endless, never-cresting wave of Russian activism. To my mind, what Putin is doing now in Syria probably reduces the risks of near-term military provocations in Europe, especially against our NATO allies. If I were a Baltic Defense Minister, I'd actually be sleeping slightly better these days.

But, we have to remember that most of us have been wrong in anticipating Russian actions in the past couple of years. Just when we thought Putin had finally realized he had acted foolishly, he then acted even more foolishly. Today, the ingredients of some future confrontation may already be coming together. After what we've seen of Russian behavior, we can't afford to be unprepared.

Mr. Chairman, members of the committee, let me close as I began, by urging realism about the problems that Russian policy creates without making those problems worse than they have to be. Many Russians understand that President Putin is damaging his own country's security as well as others. They should hear from us and from you. They should be able to speak up against his actions. They should understand that the United States will protect itself, its allies, and its interests. They should also understand that there can be a place for them in this effort if they want it.

Thank you, Mr. Chairman. I look forward to our discussion.

[The prepared statement of Ambassador Sestanovich follows:]

PREPARED STATEMENT BY STEPHEN SESTANOVICH

Chairman McCain, Senator Reed, Members of the Committee:

Thank you for the opportunity to join your discussion today on Russian policy in Europe and the Middle East, especially actions taken by Russian military units in Syria in the last few days. These Russian steps are not only unprecedented in the post-Cold War era, they have few antecedents in the Cold War itself. They call for careful analysis and an equally careful policy response.

Members of this committee surely remember how General Joe Dunford, the new JCS Chairman, described Russian policy in his confirmation testimony. "Alarming," he called it, and I completely agree. I don't, however, agree with the other thing General Dunford said. He described Russia as an "existential threat" to the United States.

Let me explain why I disagree.

First, in using this language we mislead ourselves. No matter how alarmed we are by Russia's current behavior, we use the term "existential threat" only because of its large strategic nuclear arsenal. Its many nuclear weapon are a potential threat whether our relations with Russia are good or bad, whether Russian behavior is reckless or wise. Russia has acted recklessly of late, but that has not really increased the "existential threat" General Dunford spoke of.

Second, this language also misleads the Russians. It feeds a public mood in Russia that borders on national hysteria. These days senior Russian officials often say things about the United States that are bizarre and incomprehensible. Unfortunately, hearing that we see Russia as an "existential threat"—pretty extreme language, after all—tells many Russians that our countries are on a collision course to war. Worse, it is understood by some to mean that America's leaders are preparing for this future conflict. I urge the members of this Committee to take a different approach—to challenge responsible Russians to see how strange their country's policy looks to the outside world, not to make ourselves seem equally strange.

Now, a few words about Russian policy itself. As I have said, it is both alarming and strange. We need to appreciate just how alarming it is, but we should not think it comes out of nowhere.

First, Russian actions in the Middle East reflect the doubling (and more) of their defense budget in the past 10 years. This program of modernization is still unfolding; the biggest procurement projects are ahead. As Russia's capabilities have increased, so has its anti-Western rhetoric. The official military doctrine adopted late last year identifies both NATO and the United States as threats to Russia.

Second, Russian actions reflect the new nationalism of Russian public opinion. The seizure of Crimea and continuing attempts to fragment eastern Ukraine have given this nationalist mood an angrier, more embattled tone. Russian decision-makers surely feel they can count on popular support for more assertive displays of national power, but they cannot be any surer of this than we can. There are in fact reasons to believe that Russian leaders worry about operations that might bring casualties down the road. (How else to explain the steadfast lying about the presence of Russian military personnel in Ukraine or the claim that in Syria only "volunteers" will take part in ground operations?)

Third, Russia's actions are a response, as President Obama has noted, to the weakness of the Assad regime in Syria, Russia's oldest (and now only) real ally in the region. As President Putin has made clear in Ukraine, he is prepared to make a significant military commitment to save embattled clients, no matter how shaky and illegitimate their position. But Putin acts this way in part because he thinks circumstances allow it. In Syria, several years of policy confusion by the United States and Europe have encouraged him. Had the United States imposed a no-fly zone in Syria three years ago, there would be no Russian intervention today.

Fourth, Secretary of Defense Ash Carter may well be right that Russian policy is "doomed to fail." But even in the course of failing it may do a great deal of damage, both in Syria and beyond. It should therefore be a goal of the United States and its allies to limit Russia's intervention. Continued confusion— including calls for Russia to focus its actions on defeating ISIS—will not achieve this aim.

Fifth, anyone responsible for the national security of the United States—and I certainly include the members of this Committee—should worry about where Russia's reckless behavior will lead next. We should not by any means conclude that we face an endless, never-cresting wave of activism. If anything, what Putin is doing now in Syria probably reduces the risk of near-term military provocations in Europe, especially against our NATO allies. (If I were a Baltic defense minister, I'd be sleeping slightly better these days.) But we have to remember that most of us have been wrong in anticipating Russian actions of the past couple of years. Just when we thought Putin had finally realized that he had acted foolishly, he acted even more foolishly. Today the ingredients of some future confrontation may already be coming together. After what we've seen of Russian behavior, we can't afford to be unprepared.

Mr. Chairman, let me close as I began—by urging realism about the problems Russian policy creates without making those problems worse than they have to be. Many Russians understand that President Putin is damaging his own country's security as well as others. They should hear from us—and from you. They should understand that the United States will protect itself, its allies, and its interests. They should also understand that there can be a place for them in this effort if they want it.

Thank you, Mr. Chairman. I look forward to our discussion.

Senator McCAIN. General Jones.

STATEMENT OF GENERAL JAMES L. JONES, USMC (RET.), CHAIRMAN, BRENT SCOWCROFT CENTER ON INTERNATIONAL SECURITY, ATLANTIC COUNCIL, AND FORMER NATIONAL SECURITY ADVISOR

General JONES. Thank you, Mr. Chairman, Senator Reed, members of the committee. Thank you for convening this important hearing at this very challenging and consequential juncture in America's relations with Russia and in world affairs, in general.

We are all witnessing the most recent and dangerous developments in Syria, where Mr. Putin, under the guise of fighting ISIL, is using force to advance his highly cynical campaign to prop up Bashar al-Assad. This action is merely the latest in a pattern of behavior emanating from Moscow that we had hoped ended with the Cold War. Unfortunately, as I came to learn during my tenure as National Security Advisor, the dissolution of the Warsaw Pact was an outcome that was neither cheered nor welcomed nor accepted by the current Russian President.

I've submitted a full written statement covering three areas that will hopefully be of help to the committee. The first is my view of Mr. Putin's primary motivations and goals. The second regards his strategy. And the third addresses some thoughts regarding what the United States and our allies could consider doing in response.

Mr. Chairman, in 2009, as National Security Advisor, I attended a breakfast meeting in Moscow between the then-Prime Minister Putin and our President. I left that meeting convinced of three things: first, that Mr. Putin will always be a product of his upbringing in the KGB; second, that he believes deeply that Russia was humiliated by the conclusion of the Cold War, and is wholeheartedly committed to righting what he sees as an historic injustice, the collapse of the Soviet Union; third, he clearly believes that NATO is a great evil and that his interests are best served by weakening the Transatlantic Alliance and destabilizing his western periphery.

These three views are reflected not only in Russia's revanchist foreign policy and adventures abroad, but also in the country's lack of political and economic evolution during his tenure as President, all quite similar to Cold War behavior and priorities. During President Medvedev's tenure, we genuinely hoped that he aimed to integrate Russia into the Euro-Atlantic ark and was the kind of partner with whom we could work to achieve common goals. Upon returning to the presidency, President Putin reversed much of the progress we made during the Medvedev presidency, and is now taking Russia down a very different path.

The Russian President has proven he remains a cynical Cold War hero, needing an enemy to make himself look good and deeply nostalgic for a Moscow-centric sphere of influence. His strategic objective is to reassert Russian power and prestige on his terms without regard to international principles and norms. He is willing to use force to achieve his objectives, including overturning internationally recognized boundaries and disregarding state sovereignty illustrated by the illegal annexation of the Crimea in 2014.

Despite an anemic economy debilitated by low oil prices, cronyism, and corruption, and now in a full recession, he is nonetheless consolidating his power effectively. He continues to subvert human rights, clamp down on media and free expression, fosters an environment of hostility for what is left of his political opposition, and takes intentionally stabilizing actions abroad, all the while operating a robust propaganda machine at home and abroad to make it appear that he is doing none of those things.

As outlined in my full statement, to pursue his ambitions he is employing a broad toolkit composed of major military, energy, and political elements. A very high priority for Mr. Putin, despite enormous domestic problems, is strengthening and modernizing the Russian military to reassert power on the world stage. United States military leaders fear that the extensive new capabilities President Putin is accumulating are being used to pursue an anti-access area-denial strategy against NATO, particularly in the Baltic Sea regions from Kaliningrad in the Black Sea region, from Russia's buildup in the Crimea, now in Syria from its deployment of anti-aircraft capabilities, and the naval bombardment from the Caspian.

There was growing concern within the alliance that President Putin is using a series of capability deployments in these sensitive areas to raise the risk, or perceived risk, of U.S. or coalition military action in these regions. We see this in Syria, where Russia's deployments are geared not towards fighting the Islamic State of Iraq and the Levant (ISIL), but rather towards protecting the regime of Assad. I believe that the Russian President's deployment of combat aircraft and sophisticated air defenses, which are not needed to fight ISIS, are intended to deter the United States-led coalition from establishing a no-fly zone in northern Syria.

Russian military exercises, some conducted on very short notice and as discussed by the other witnesses, also pose a significant cause for concern. Major military maneuvers in the Arctic, joined with China in naval drills near our Japanese allies, and held major—and major exercises, which included tens of thousands of troops, on NATO's eastern flank. Indeed, in March of 2015, Russia held an exercise intended to simulate the invasion of Denmark and the Baltic states. In some cases, the guise of training has been used to mask long-term Russian troop deployments, such as in Syria last month and in eastern Ukraine, where the United States European Command has estimated there may be as many as 12,000 Russian troops. Russia's use of so-called ''volunteers,'' or ''little green men,'' which ostensibly offer Moscow plausible deniability, is another element of the Kremlin's so-called ''hybrid warfare'' tactic. We have been alerted by Moscow that such volunteers may find their way to Syria very soon. There have also—we have—there have also—we have also seen the deployment of more aggressive and more capable Russian naval forces.

Finally, there are increasing reports that Russian military aircraft are violating NATO airspace with their transponders turned off, raising the risk of civilian aircraft accidents while violating the sovereignty of our treaty allies. NATO intercepted some 400 Russian aircraft flying over Europe in 2014. A number suggest that 2015 will exceed that total. And, of course, just this week, Russia violated the sovereign airspace of our Turkish allies.

There is another weapon that Mr. Putin has been utilizing to satisfy his ambitions for quite some time, and that is energy, energy by seeking to maintain European dependence on Russian gas and use it as a lever to—for manipulation. The members of this committee understand that Mr. Putin's incursion in the Crimea is, among other things, about exercising political power through the control of energy and about brandishing the threat of energy scarcity to intimidate and manipulate vulnerable populations. Fortunately, Europe is now awakening to the threat and is investing in redundancies, gas storage hubs, and interconnectors that reduce Russia's ability to hold countries hostage.

Thirdly, President Putin is working hard to sow division within the western alliance and undercut the cohesion of the Euro-Atlantic ark of economic and security cooperation. He has built links to European party leaders on the far right and far left in order to foster close relationships at the political and financial levels, and made a habit of sustaining old and corrupt alliances, such as with Syrian President Assad. Just this week, President Assad noted the importance of the Russia, Iran, Iraq alliance that's sustaining his regime.

So, before us is emerging one of the premier strategic challenges of the post-Cold War period, and that is doing what we can do to counter President Putin's retrograde ambitions in favor of the peaceful and progressive order of the transatlantic community that the world had envisioned at the opening of the 21st century.

In the face of the strategic environment I've described, I believe the United States should lead the alliance in developing a three-pronged approach that includes economic, political, and security components:

First, in the economic realm, to underline Mr. Putin's use of energy as a political weapon, the United States should support the European Union's development of an energy, telecommunications, and transportation infrastructure corridor along a north-south axis from the Baltic to the Adriatic. My full statement provides greater details on this major strategic initiative, and I ask permission to submit for the record a comprehensive plan for doing so.

Senator MCCAIN. Without objection.

General JONES. I have a copy of the plan right here.

Senator MCCAIN. Without objection.

General JONES. There is much we can do, and must do, to support the development of this critical infrastructure to complete Europe and counter Mr. Putin's use of energy as a weapon. So, I would ask your permission, Mr. Chairman, to make the report a part of the hearing record.

Senator MCCAIN. Without objection.

General JONES. Thank you.

I recommend the Transatlantic Trade and Investment Partnership to promote transatlantic growth, prosperity, and security making the alliance resilient and certainly more unified. And we should maintain U.S./EU sanctions imposed in response to Russia's illegal actions in the Ukraine. These sanctions may not have altered Putin's strategic calculus in the Ukraine, but they have raised a cost to his actions and left Russia partially economically isolated.

Secondly, politically, a central tenet of United States strategy for countering Russia should be to strengthen transatlantic solidarity and cooperation. American leadership in this effort will be crucial in fostering a common vision for the alliance in the face of new and more challenging operating environments. This should be accompanied by a comprehensive public diplomacy campaign spotlighting the values that make the transatlantic community unique and conducive to human development: free and open markets, respect for human rights and democratic governance, respect for the rule of law—values that stand today in stark contrast to Mr. Putin's Russia.

Part of that effort must be to reaffirm NATO's open-door policy. At next year's summit in Warsaw, NATO should admit Montenegro, assuming it has met all political and military commitments. Doing so would counter Russia's growing influence in the Balkans and send a powerful signal that the vision of a united Europe whole and free remains viable. A similar effort should be made by Washington to unlock the tragic political conflict within the alliance that has prevented Macedonia from taking its rightful place as a NATO member.

Third, the security mission. We must enhance NATO force presence in an eastern Europe to include American forces. This will be controversial, because some allies now fear provoking Russia, which will require careful diplomacy. Given Russia's aggressive exercises and troop positioning on NATO's eastern flank, I believe we run a greater risk of conflict by not increasing NATO's presence in central and eastern Europe. NATO, Mr. Chairman, must become more proactive, more agile within the alliance in order to prevent future conflict. I applaud the efforts of the

United States Congress to fund the President's $1 billion initiative to enhance the presence of United States rotational forces, air policing, and infrastructure in central eastern and southeast Europe. This appropriation should continue, given the ongoing Russian threat to our allies, but United States political leaders should also press our allies to continue their own contributions to NATO's readiness action plan. The next summit in Warsaw will be critical to the future of the alliance.

I've offered additional suggestions in my full statement. They include making resilience a core task of NATO to complement the NATO's—the alliance's current core task of collective defense, cooperative security, and crisis management, enhancing NATO's cybersecurity capabilities and responsibilities, empowering the Supreme Allied Commander to conduct rapid troop deployment in response to Russia's reliance on strategic surprise and hybrid warfare, and providing robust and well-targeted assistance to the Ukraine.

I support the administration's recent decisions on long-range counter-battery radars to Ukraine. I believe we should take additional measures, such as providing the anti-tank missiles, communications, and intelligence support, training in counter-electronic warfare capabilities that have been requested by Kyiv and are in the 2016 NDAA.

With the committee's permission, I would like to submit two items for the hearing record containing proposals by the Atlantic Council for steps the U.S. Government could consider in responding to President Putin's actions to assist our friends and allies in eastern Europe.

Mr. Chairman, Senator Reed, and members of the committee, let me close by saying that we have all been deeply disappointed by Russia's actions in Syria, the Ukraine, and in eastern Europe, and the negative effect these actions have had on our bilateral relationship. I believe these actions merit careful considerations of the tough response that all of us have outlined.

Having said that, President Putin will not be in power forever. There will be a Russia beyond him. The United States and our allies should continue to make clear to the Russian people that we believe that Russia has its rightful place in a united Europe whole and free and at peace, provided that Russia is willing to respect the sovereignty and the free will of its neighbors, demonstrate a commitment to democracy and human rights, and respect the rules of the road in the international system.

Mr. Chairman, thank you for allowing me the opportunity to testify before you today, and I look forward to answering any questions you may have.

[The prepared statement of General Jones follows:]

PREPARED TESTIMONY BY GENERAL JAMES L. JONES, USMC (RET.)

Mr. Chairman, Ranking Member Reed, and Members of the Committee, thank you for convening this important hearing at this very challenging and consequential juncture in America's relations with Russia, and in world affairs.

We have all witnessed the most recent and dangerous developments in Syria where Mr. Putin, under the guise of fighting ISIL, is using force to advance his highly cynical campaign to prop up Bashar al-Assad. This action is merely the latest in a pattern of behavior emanating from Moscow that we had hoped ended with the Cold War. Unfortunately, as I came to learn during my tenure as National Security Advisor, the dissolution of the Warsaw Pact was an outcome neither cheered nor accepted by the current Russian president.

I would like to share with the committee my thoughts on three dimensions of the situation before us. First, I will describe my view of Mr. Putin's primary motivations, which go a long way toward explaining his actions in the Middle East, Europe, and Ukraine; second, I will touch on the strategy he is employing to achieve his objectives; and third I will conclude by sharing my own recommendations for steps that the United States and our allies should consider in response to Mr. Putin's activities.

PUTIN'S WORLD VIEW AND DOMESTIC SITUATION

In 2009, I attended a breakfast meeting between President Obama and President Putin. I left that breakfast convinced of three things: first, Mr. Putin is a product of his upbringing in the KGB; second, he believes deeply that Russia was humiliated by the conclusion of the Cold War and is wholeheartedly committed to 'righting' what he sees as an historic injustice, the collapse of the Soviet Union. Third, he clearly believes that NATO is a great evil and that his interests are best served by weakening the transatlantic alliance and destabilizing his western periphery. These three views are reflected not only in Russia's revanchist foreign policy, but also in the country's lack of political and economic evolution under his tenure as President.

As national security advisor, we worked hard with President Obama and the Russian President at that time, Mr. Medvedev, on advancing the United States–Russia relationship to a new paradigm. I genuinely believed that President Medvedev aimed to integrate Russia into the Euro-Atlantic arc and was the kind of partner with whom we could achieve common goals. We made important progress including the START II treaty; convincing Russia to withhold its delivery of S–300 surface to air missiles to Iran during a key period of time; and achieving their cooperation on a range of non-traditional security challenges on regional matters such as Afghanistan and transnational crime. Unfortunately, upon returning to the Kremlin, President Putin reversed much of the modest progress we made during the Medvedev presidency, and moved Russia down a very different path, away from Euro-Atlantic integration of his predecessor.

President Putin has proven he remains a cynical cold warrior, deeply nostalgic for a Russian-centric sphere of influence. In addition, Russia's recent military involvement in Syria and increased cooperation with Iran, combined with greater political engagement across the Middle East, indicates Mr. Putin is upping its effort to increase Russian influence in that region as well.

Mr. Putin's strategic objective is equally clear: to reassert Russian power and prestige on his terms. International principles and norms of behavior are not in his calculus. He is willing to use force to achieve his objectives, including overturning internationally recognized boundaries and disregarding state sovereignty, illustrated by the illegal annexation of Crimea in 2014.

Given his ambitions and actions, Mr. Putin is far more interested in modernizing his military than reforming Russia's dysfunctional and corrupt political and economic systems. Low oil prices and western sanctions have negatively impacted the country's already fetid business environment and placed great strain on the Russian economy.

While Mr. Putin's poll numbers ostensibly remain quite high in Russia, particularly after the annexation of Crimea—it is difficult to know if these numbers are credible given the lack of civil society, free media, political opposition and independent institutions in Russia. But for now he is consolidating power effectively.

It remains to be seen if his popularity can survive the kind of significant economic downturn which Russia is experiencing. The country is now in full recession for the first time in six years. The World Bank forecasts Russia's economy will shrink by 3.8 percent in 2015.

Russia's political system and human rights situation has also degraded during Mr. Putin's return to the Kremlin. The Russian state actively persecutes homosexuals, has clamped down on media and free expression, has fostered an environment of hostility to what is left of the political opposition and free media, and operates a robust propaganda machine.

PUTIN'S INTERNATIONAL OBJECTIVES AND MODUS OPERANDI

Russia's aggressiveness abroad is not only a means of diverting attention from his domestic shortcomings; it emanates naturally from President Putin's world view and his desire to project power and influence. In my view, Putin aims to restore Russia as a major player in the international system; to leverage Russia's strengths and enemies' perceived weaknesses to his advantage; to harness a resurgent nationalism for his adventures; to sow division within the transatlantic alliance and on a larger scale, disrupt international order.

Military Action

Strengthening and modernizing the Russian military has been central to Mr. Putin's ambition of reasserting Russian power on the world stage. Russia is presently halfway through a ten-year, $700 billion defense modernization initiative that is projected to result in the acquisition of 1,100 helicopters, 100 ships (including 24 submarines), 2,300 tanks, and 2,000 artillery pieces. While President Putin has looked to protect the military from budget cuts due to low oil prices, there are signs the modernization process may be forced to move at a slower pace.

Even so, United States military leaders fear these new capabilities are being used to pursue an anti-access/area denial strategy against NATO, particularly in the Baltic Sea region from Kaliningrad; in the Black Sea region from Russia's buildup in Crimea; and now in Syria from its deployment of anti-aircraft capabilities. There is growing concern within the alliance that Putin is using a series of capability deployments in these sensitive areas to raise the risk, or perceived risk of United States or coalition military action in these regions. We see this in Syria, where Russia's deployments are geared not toward fighting ISIL but rather toward protecting the murderous regime of Bashar al-Assad. I believe that the Russian President's deployment of combat aircraft and sophisticated air defenses – which are not needed to fight ISIS—are intended to deter the United States-led coalition from establishing a no-fly zone in northern Syria.

In addition to investments in Russian military equipment, large-scale Russian military exercises, some conducted on very short notice are a cause for concern. Russia has held major exercises in the Arctic, joined with China in naval drills near our Japanese allies, and held major exercises which included tens of thousands of troops on NATO's eastern flank. Indeed, in March 2015, Russia held an exercise intended to simulate the invasion of Denmark and the Baltic states.

In some cases, exercises have been used to mask long-term Russian troop deployments, such as in Syria last month and in Eastern Ukraine, where United States European command has estimated there may be as many as 12,000–Russian troops. Russia's use of so-called 'volunteers' or little green men – which ostensibly offer Moscow plausible deniability – is another element of the Kremlin's so-called 'hybrid warfare tactics.' We have been alerted by Moscow that such 'volunteers' may find their way to Syria very soon.

There is real concern among allies in northeast Europe that a snap exercise could be used as the pretext for Russian forces to suddenly conduct a small-scale incursion into NATO territory that would create a *fait accompli*, or risk all-out war with Moscow. This would be a direct challenge to Article V of the Washington treaty, and potentially end the principle of collective defense which is the very heart of NATO's founding treaty. Given the growing anti-access capabilities described above, that cost could be high indeed if we and our allies are unprepared for such an outcome.

There have also seen the deployment of more aggressive and more capable Russian naval forces. As stated by the Commander of United States Naval Forces Europe, the Russians are constructing an "arc of steel from the Arctic to the Mediterranean. Starting with their new Arctic bases, to Leningrad in the Baltic and Crimea in the Black Sea, Russia has introduced advanced air defense, cruise missile systems and new platforms." As evidenced by recent Russian naval activity, Mr. Putin is focusing his naval capability on addressing the perceived advantages of NATO navies. He is signaling to us that the maritime domain is contested.

Finally, there are increasing reports that Russian military aircraft are violating NATO airspace with their transponders off, raising the risk of civilian aircraft accidents while violating the sovereignty of our treaty allies. NATO intercepted some 400 Russian aircraft flying over Europe in 2014 and numbers suggest that 2015 will exceed that total. And of course, just this week we saw Russia violate the airspace of our Turkish allies.

Russia's advanced cyber capabilities are also a source of grave concern for the United States and its allies. We have seen Russia employ its impressive cyber capabilities against Estonia, a treaty ally. We must be alert to Moscow's willingness to use this tool to achieve its political goals.

Energy Action

Mr. Putin's strategy does not rely on military power alone. He seeks to maintain European dependence on Russian gas and continues to use that dependence as a weapon; he deftly applies a 'divide and conquer' strategy to undermine Europe's cohesion. We see this in particular through the Nord-Stream pipeline, which connects Russia directly to Europe while bypassing Ukraine. Also in Russia's gas pricing tactics which reward its friends and punishes its opponents. The members of this committee understand that Mr. Putin's incursion in the Crimea is, among other things, about exercising political power through the control of energy, and about brandishing the threat of energy scarcity to intimidate and manipulate vulnerable populations. The greater the gap between global supply and demand, the more destructive the energy weapon will become.

While Russian troops occupy a sovereign country, including a major port, to stop Ukraine from receiving energy imports, Mr. Putin's rubles are being spent on campaigns to stop natural gas development in central Europe—all with a mind towards creating scarcity, dependence, and vulnerability among countries who are U.S. friends, allies, and trading partners.

Fortunately, Europe is awakening to the threat and is investing in redundancies, gas storage hubs, and interconnectors that reduce Russia's ability to hold countries hostage.

Political Action

An important part of Russia's foreign policy is to sow division within the western alliance and to undercut the cohesion of the Euro-Atlantic arc of economic and security cooperation. Moscow actively courts EU countries that are economically weak or dependent on trade with Russia in hopes of fracturing unity. This past summer Putin unsuccessfully wooed the newly elected Syriza government in Greece in the midst of ongoing discussions with the Eurozone over its economic rescue package in hopes of convincing Athens to vote against EU sanctions on Russia.

Russia has also built links to European party leaders on the far right and far left in order to foster close relationships at the political and financial levels, such as with the National Front in France. Mr. Putin has made a habit of sustaining old and corrupt alliances (such as with Syrian President Assad or Belarussian President Lukashenko). Just this week, President Assad noted the importance of the Russia-Iran-Iraq alliance at sustaining his regime.

State-controlled media outlets spread untruths primarily with the intent to undermine western diplomacy and messaging, mask Russia's aggressive intentions, and plant seeds of doubt within western publics. Russian television parrots the government's narrative that Russia is under attack from Ukrainian 'fascists,' a hostile NATO, and ISIL. The Russian government deliberately lies about Russia's activities in Ukraine and denies it has forces there, despite visual proof to the contrary. It has also obfuscated the role of Russian-backed rebels in downing Malaysian airlines flight 17, and has outrageously blocked a UN tribunal to get the facts. Let's not forget that 298 souls lost their lives in this unconscionable tragedy. Yet Russia thumbs its nose at the international community by blocking simple fact finding – a stunning example of how out of touch its behavior is with international norms and standards of justice. More recently, Russian has lied about the fact that Russian the air force is currently bombing United States-backed opposition groups in Syria, claiming instead that they are striking at ISIS despite evidence to the contrary.

Actionable Recommendations for Countering Russian Aggression

In the face of the strategic environment I have described, I believe the United States should lead its allies in developing a three-pronged approach that includes economic, political, and security components.

Economic considerations:

Invest in North-South Energy Infrastructure in Europe: To undermine Putin's use of energy as a political weapon, the United States should support the EU's development of energy, tele-communications, and transportation infrastructure along a North-South axis from the Baltic to the Adriatic Sea. This North-South corridor would constitute the most strategically viable alternative to Russia's regional abuse of current energy supplies and supply routes; foster greater cohesion among Central and East European states; undermine Russia's monopoly on energy pricing; and severely inhibit its ability to use energy as a weapon. Along with my Polish colleague Pawel Olechnowicz, CEO of the Grupa Lotus, I have co-chaired an Atlantic Council report exploring this issue in greater detail. It includes a set of recommendation receiving strong support in Europe and the United States. There is much we can and must do to support the development of this critical infrastructure. I would ask your permission to make the report a part of the hearing record.

TTIP (Transatlantic Trade and Investment Partnership): Energy security is instrumental for a transatlantic growth, prosperity, and security. The same can be said of successfully concluding TTIP. Europe and the United States have the largest trading partnership in the world. Strengthening it serves our mutual interests and reaffirms the centrality of the transatlantic alliance in the 21st century. TTIP also affords the U.S. a unique opportunity to author the rulebook and roadmap for 21st century advanced economies, which would stand in stark contrast with Russia's reliance upon crony capitalism.

Maintain U.S.-EU Sanctions: The sanctions regime that was implemented in response to Russia's illegal actions in Ukraine may not have altered Putin's strategic calculus in Ukraine, but they have raised a cost to his actions and left Russia economically isolated. The United States and EU should maintain Russian sanctions until full military and political implementation of the Minsk II agreement has been secured in Ukraine, and should also be prepared to increase sanctions if Minsk II isn't fully implemented (Moscow must be made aware that its support for rebels will incur increasingly costly penalties). Furthermore, Russia's full implementation of the Minsk II agreement shouldn't necessarily result in 'business as usual' either; Crimea-related sanctions should remain in place until Russian forces evacuate the Crimean peninsula and return it to Ukraine.

Political Considerations:

Maintain transatlantic solidarity: A central tenet of a United States strategy for countering Russia should be to strengthen transatlantic solidarity and cooperation. American leadership in this effort will be crucial and fostering a common vision for the alliance in the face of a new and more challenging operating environment

A second component of our political strategy should be a comprehensive public diplomacy campaign spotlighting the values that make the transatlantic community unique and conducive to human development: free and open markets; respect for human rights and democratic governance; and respect for the rule of law—values that stand in stark contrast to Putin's Russia.

A key source of Russia's influence is its predation of fragile governments and the exercise of corrupt practices. The United States must continue to support ongoing political reforms in Europe, particularly in countries on the NATO/EU periphery such as Moldova, Georgia, Ukraine, and the Balkan states that are currently seeking closer association with Euro-Atlantic institutions.

Reaffirm NATO's open door policy: NATO must prevent Russia from shutting its long-standing 'open door' membership policy. At next year's NATO summit in Warsaw, NATO should admit Montenegro (assuming it has met all political and military commitments). Doing so would counter Russia's growing influence in the Balkans and send a powerful signal that the vision of a united Europe, whole and free, remains viable. A similar effort should be made by Washington to unlock the tragic political conflict within the alliance that has prevented Macedonia from taking its rightful place as a NATO member.

Security considerations:

Enhance NATO force presence in Central Europe: The United States should rally allies around a permanent NATO force presence in Central and Eastern Europe, to include American forces. This will be controversial because some allies fear provocation of Russia, which will require careful American diplomacy. Given Russia's aggressive exercises and troop positioning on NATO's eastern flank, I believe we run a greater risk of conflict by NOT increasing NATO's presence in Central and Eastern Europe.

Maintain funding for the European Reassurance Initiative: I applaud the efforts of the U.S. Congress to fund the President's $1 billion initiative to enhance the presence of U.S. rotational forces, air policing, and infrastructure in Central, Eastern, and Southeast Europe. This appropriation should continue, given the ongoing Russian threat to our allies, but United States political leaders should also press our allies to continue their own contributions to NATO's Readiness Action Plan.

Make Resilience a core task of NATO: A key element of Russia's strategy is the use of strategic surprise and hybrid threats to take advantage of weak states. Adding resilience as a core task would complement NATO's current core tasks of collective defense, cooperative security, and crisis management. An important component of building greater resilience should be enhancing NATO's cybersecurity capabilities and responsibilities.

Provide security assistance to Ukraine: I support the Administration's recent decision to send long-range counter-battery radars to Ukraine and believe we should take additional measures, such as providing the anti-tank missiles, intelligence support, training and counter-electronic warfare capabilities that have been requested by Kiev and mandated by the 2016 NDAA.

Empower the SACEUR to make rapid troop deployments: Russia's reliance on strategic surprise and hybrid warfare, illustrated by the seizure of Crimea, poses acute risks for our NATO allies such as the Baltic States. They in turn fear a Russian snap exercise that could potentially result in encroachment on their territorial sovereignty. To counter this threat, NATO must empower the SACEUR to employ his best military judgment and order rapid troop deployments in the interest of Alliance security.

With the Committee's permission, I would like to submit two items for the hearing record containing proposals by the Atlantic Council for steps the United States government should consider in responding to President Putin's actions and assisting our friends and allies in eastern Europe.

Mr. Chairman, Ranking Member Reed, and members of the committee, let me close by saying that I have been deeply disappointed by Russia's actions in Syria, Ukraine, and Eastern Europe, and the negative effect these actions have had on the United States–Russian relationship. I believe these actions merit the tough response I have outlined.

Having said that, President Putin will not be in power forever. There will be a Russia beyond him. The United States and its allies should continue to make clear to the Russian people that they believe Russia has its rightful place in a united Europe, whole, free, and at peace, provided that Russia is willing to respect the sovereignty and free will of its neighbors, demonstrate a commitment to democracy and human rights, and respect the rules of the road in the international system.

Thank you for allowing me to testify before you today. I look forward to answering any questions you may have.

Senator MCCAIN. Well, I thank you.

And I thank the witnesses.

After the Russian general knocked on the door of our embassy to notify us that we had an hour notice that Russian airstrikes would begin in Syria, the President said he wasn't going to engage in a proxy war. Secretary Kerry said this was an opportunity. And our Secretary of Defense said that this was, quote, "unprofessional." And, in response—and, of course, deconfliction is our hot—top priority. Obviously, that hasn't happened. And now we're—the United States is rerouting its flights to avoid Russian warplanes, not the opposite.

I'm curious what kind of signal that sends. And, far more importantly, this cruise missile strike, I think, has dimensions and significance that may be, in a short time, lost on us, because I think it is a seminal event when a country launches cruise missiles from 900 miles away on a target that—on targets that are the people that we have supported, trained, and equipped, and sent in to fight.

So, I guess my question is—two. One, what is the overall significance of this latest Russian escalation? And what does it—signal does it send to anybody that we would train, equip, and send into combat that we're going to sit by and watch them slaughtered by the Russians?

General Keane?

General KEANE. Yeah. Mr. Chairman, the introduction of the cruise missiles is a—is testimony to the loss of precision-guided munitions and missile technology advantage that we've had for 25 years. For some time now, the Chinese missile development strategy, the Iranian missile development strategy, and what Russia is doing also with missiles and precision-guided munitions, have literally caught up to the technological advantage that we've had. And certainly this is the first manifestation of it. We are the country that used cruise missiles on our adversaries, and certainly Russians have had this capability, and they're obviously using it. So, we have to understand that, that that technological advantage that we've had is gone. And it's in countries that we're in competition with; that is, Iran, China, and Russia.

In terms of the provocation, you know, I'm absolutely convinced that Russia—you know, the psychological bully that they are with a national chip on their shoulder since the collapse of the Soviet Union in '91, I believe they are absolutely convinced they can have their way with us. And this campaign that they're doing in Syria was certainly calculated with that thought in mind. When you think about it, this is—as I said in my opening line, it's unprecedented for them to move this distance, establish an airbase in another country that, for their purposes, is isolated and vulnerable, from a military perspective. But, they established this base with confidence that they will be able to control the airspace that they want to use, that the United States will not impede any of their air operations and their support for ground operations. And they calculated that, and I—and it turned out to be the case.

Not only have they done that, but much as we're doing in China, who is building airbases in archipelagos in the South China Sea, as opposed to flying over those bases and—because they're international waters, we're avoiding them. So, right now, air operations in Iraq is avoidance operations. We have an enemy, called the Islamic State of Iraq and Syria (ISIS), but we're now—that enemy, called ISIS in Syria, because of Russian control of the airspace and desire to fly wherever they want, when they want, we're avoiding that. And what we should have said right from the outset is that,

''We're going to fly our airplanes wherever we want, when we want, and what you should do''——

Senator MCCAIN. And what's your——

General KEANE.—''is avoid that, or else face confrontation,'' and put our foot down.

Senator MCCAIN. And what——

General KEANE. And we're doing the opposite. And I think they recognize that.

Senator MCCAIN. And what is your response when, as I received just last night from—on one of the television shows, ''That means you want war with Russia, Senator McCain.'' Do you want war with Russia, General Keane?

General KEANE. Of course not. But, I think there are prudent actions that you can take to discourage an ally. If we—the other calculation that Russia has made, and it's been manifested as a result of the red line in Syria, the annexation of Crimea, the movement into Ukraine, and a sort of deniability that he gives his adversaries by the kinds of deceptive ways he uses military force—I mean, I believe his calculation—and it's a correct one—is that we get paralyzed by the fear of escalation and by the fear of confrontation. And he understands that. And he uses that to his advantage. And he's going to continue to do it.

And I'm absolutely convinced—I disagree with the Ambassador—I don't believe the Syria operation in any way, shape, or form will hold him back for exerting his national interests in the Baltics and eastern Europe and breaking down the strategic buffer that he clearly wants to have. And he will use this—I'm convinced of it—as a platform and foundation for more aggression against that buffer in eastern Europe. And he——

Senator MCCAIN. Ms. Conley.

General KEANE.—will do it because he knows he can and because he knows he will get away with it.

Senator MCCAIN. Ms. Conley.

Ms. CONLEY. I think President Putin has now clearly said that there will be no international regime change, based on his understanding of the Libya operation in 2011, where the U.N. Security Council basically, in his view, gave a green light to changing regime. He is a status quo power, and the power he is the most concerned about, as Ambassador Sestanovich said, is his own power and maintaining his own power. But, that also projects to other powers. And so, I think right now this is his strongest message.

He is also sending a clear message to President Obama that he is not a regional power, he is a global power, and he has extensive reach. And I think, again, the cruise missiles demonstrate.

We're also seeing where Russia's military modernization and its significant increases in its defense spending has paid off. It can move quickly, and it does have sophisticated weaponry that it can use. And I think we're seeing that. And for countries that are quite interested in purchasing Russian equipment, this is also a benefit of seeing the level of sophistication that it has and will be willing to sell.

Mr. Putin acknowledges strength, and he exploits weakness. And our Syrian policy has been a demonstration of lack of resolve and weakness, of which he has been able to exploit. Now, there—in some ways, in talking to some of my Polish and central European colleagues, you know, they're advocating, ''Please, send two Russian divisions to Syria. Get the heat off of my border and bog Syria—bog the Russians down in Syria.'' But, this—he can move very quickly, and he can turn the temperature up when he needs, and temperature down. And this is where we are constantly reacting to his agenda. We're getting out of his way. We have not set a strategic framework to say, ''These are what our rules''——

And I would just finally say, last year President Putin, in his address to the Valdai Discussion Club, his speech was entitled ''The World Order: New Rules or a Game Without Rules?'' His rules. This is Putin's rules. And he's making us work with his game. And I think we have to return to our rules, which were established at the end of the second World War, international legal norms. And that's what we have to get back to.

Senator MCCAIN. Ambassador?

Ambassador SESTANOVICH. Thank you, Senator.

You know, I think General Keane is right about something very important, and that is, this is a kind of situation that we didn't face in the Cold War. Because, in the Cold War, there was a kind of constraint on Russian—Soviet activity, because they—as you say, General—feared escalation. Since the Cold War, American use of military power has actually been almost entirely free of a fear of Russian interference. And what Putin has done is change that. He's said, ''You cannot act independently anymore without worrying about my actions.'' And he's been the first mover in this case. I don't think the difference is so much a technological one as a political one. He has backfooted us by taking the first action and saying, ''You deconflict with me.'' Obviously, our preference would be for him to think he had to deconflict with us. So, that——

Senator MCCAIN. Classic example of this is the air operations.

Ambassador SESTANOVICH. That is a very big change. We now are being told by the Russians, ''We're going to be free to act independently without being checked by you.'' That's—that is not only something we haven't experienced since the end of the Cold War, it really is a change, even from the Cold War itself.

But, I think we should not forget what some of our advantages are here. I think our discussion has been very bilateral, as though it's us against the Russians, forgetting——

Senator MCCAIN. Could I—I'm way——

Ambassador SESTANOVICH. Yeah.

Chairman MCCAIN.—over my time.

Ambassador SESTANOVICH. Yeah.

Senator MCCAIN. If you could——

Ambassador SESTANOVICH. I just want to—I—let me finish the thought.

Senator MCCAIN. Okay, sure.

Ambassador SESTANOVICH. We have, in Europe and in the Middle East, an array of states that want to work with us, and who, working with us, can actually check the Russians and limit this kind of independent action. One of the big things about our passive Syria policy over the past several years is that we've not done anything in the way of coalition management to create a block of states that would keep the Russians out.

Senator McCain. Thank you.

General Jones, could you hold your answer? Because I'm way over time, and——

Senator Reed. No, go ahead.

Senator McCain. All right, please go ahead, General Jones.

General Jones. Very quickly.

I think we've been off balance in Syria since Assad violated the red lines and used chemical and biological weapons on his own people. The penalty for that should have been quick and decisive. Many people advocated—I was one of them—that a no-fly zone and a safety zone for refugees be created in Syria. And it went along with international cooperation.

I think where we are now is that Putin is basically offering a trade, "Assad stays in power and then we'll take care of ISIL." And I think that's really what it boils down to. I think we should consider really elevating NATO in this, an emergency meeting of the North Atlantic Council, to shore up and demonstrate the alliance's resolve, not only for eastern Europe, but also in the current Middle Eastern problem.

Thank you.

Senator McCain. Senator Reed.

Senator Reed. Well, thank you very much, Mr. Chairman.

General Jones, in your testimony, you touched very, I think, insightfully on the whole issue of energy policy. We have a very contentious and confrontational Russia right now at $50 a barrel in oil. If it swings back to $100 a barrel, we could be in real dire straits. So, that raises a huge issue, which I don't think that we're going to settle here at this panel, but we should be thinking strategically, in terms of, How do we, in the world market, maintain a lower price of oil? Because that's what, basically, will take away a lot of his ability to be confrontational. Is that fair?

General Jones. Senator Reed, I really believe in this and the fact that the United States still does not have a strategic energy policy, I—there isn't one that I can find anywhere that's written, either classified or unclassified. This is a—an asset in our quiver that is incredible, in terms of future potential. And the sooner, I think, that we understand that energy security is a vital part of our toolkit, in terms of deciding what we're going to do and not going to do in the rest of the world, I don't think we fully grasp how the energy situation has changed the power balance in the world.

Mr. Putin relied on that. He—it's now—he's paid an economic price for it. I think there are ways in which, with United States leadership, particularly with Europe, that we can continue to help our friends and allies wean themselves off of their dependence on Russian energy, which is—will continue to create his economic isolation.

Senator Reed. Let me ask you another question, General Jones. As the National Security Advisor, I assume you wrestled with this issue, which is: Many of the proposals, in terms of countering the Assad regime, would require overt attacks against Assad's forces. Do we have the legal authority to do that? Most of what we've done, legally, has been under the AUMF, which has been in effect for more than a decade. But, do—are there legal problems that the

President would confront if he, in fact, decided he was going to take more dramatic action?

General JONES. In direct confrontation——

Senator REED. With Syria.

General JONES. I'm sure there are.

Senator REED. Yeah.

General JONES. I'm sure there are.

Senator REED. So, the——

General JONES. But, those—but, that's—that doesn't mean we shouldn't confront them and resolve them.

Senator REED. I absolutely——

General JONES. Yeah.

Senator REED.—agree.

General JONES. Right.

Senator REED. I think that, in many cases, the debates—assumes that these are policy issues alone, that they can be done by decision——

General JONES. Right.

Senator REED.—immediately, where, in fact, there are—I think we have to be very careful. I know Senator McCain has been extraordinarily eloquent about the issues involving legal authorities and they can use—when we can use them, how do they constrain us, how do they enable us. But, let me thank you.

I'll—finally, and I will ask for a quick response, and I'll ask the Ambassador and then I'll—anyone else wants to chime in. The decisive ability to change the facts on the ground in Syria is somehow ground forces, in my view. I don't think airpower alone, by any side, is going to decisively sort of settle the issue. When it comes to the Russian engagement, they have several options, but the three primary options would be to rely on the Syrian forces that are there with their air support; second, to use Russian advisors, command-and-control apparatus, but not troops, with their airpower; and a third would be, as—there's been some suggestions of Russian formations, et cetera.

Mr. Ambassador, just your comments on those options. Would they be used? Is there something we're missing?

Ambassador SESTANOVICH. Senator, to work through those in exactly the order you suggest, hoping not to get to number three, but for Russian officials already to be mentioning volunteers suggests to me we should worry that that's already entrain, and that their analysis is, they can't succeed without it. If that's what it takes to succeed, I think there could be some deployments, and maybe not too far down the road.

Senator REED. Any other comments by the panelists? Ms. Conley? General Keane?

General KEANE. Yeah. I think they're going to wait a little bit. They know full well that IRGC is with Syrian army units. They know that the IRGC is leading, in some cases, the local militia, but, in all cases, advising them. And they also know that there's about 7,000 Hezbollah and about 3,000 Iraqi Shi'a militia that are being returned from Iraq. They were there in greater numbers at one time or another. Russian doesn't—Russia doesn't have a clue whether this ground force is going to be effective or not. And I think they're going to wait to see if they have to inject something.

And then if they do, I think they would go through an escalation of advisors and other things before they would actually put direct combats.

Listen, Putin is no fool, here. He's got Afghanistan in his rear-view mirror, 10 years—a 10-year commitment that really hurt his country and lost confidence of his people in the national decision authority, et cetera. So, I think they will be guarded about their introduction of significant combat forces.

Senator REED. Thank you.

Thank you, Mr. Chairman.

Senator MCCAIN. Senator Inhofe.

Senator INHOFE. Thank you, Mr. Chairman.

I'd—first of all, I really appreciate the very blunt answers we're getting here. And we've been getting them in this committee for quite a while now. We had—not just General Dunford, but others—Clapper—coming in and making statements that I think are really pretty courageous and talking about the seriousness that we're facing right now.

When the Ambassador mentioned—and I was prepared to ask this question before, because I'm reading from the Council of Foreign Relations now that you had disagreed with General Dunford in this respect. And I noticed three nervous people while you were saying that. I'd like to have each one respond as to whether or not you agree with the statement of General Dunford, in terms of the existential seriousness of this.

Senator MCCAIN. Ladies first.

Ms. CONLEY. Thank you. Well, I—what I understood is, General Dunford's statement was that Russia is the only power that can wipe the United States off the planet with its nuclear arsenal.

Senator INHOFE. Let me interrupt you to——

Ms. CONLEY. Yeah.

Senator INHOFE.—say what he said to this committee. It was—and this is a quote—he said, ''Russia presents the greatest threat to our national security.''

Ms. CONLEY. And I think, based on their ability and as well as the focus that we have seen over the last several years on strengthening and modernizing their nuclear strategic deterrent and their nuclear submarine forces. And I think, also, because we have seen, over the last several years, beginning in 2008 with the Russian invasion of Georgia, that the Kremlin is fully able and willing to use military means to accomplish its political objectives. It is not—you know, it does not believe it will be prevented. Now, that's within its own neighborhood.

So, I think that is why the Chairman of the Joint Chiefs of Staff is very concerned about Russian activities and aggression and their willingness to use their——

Senator INHOFE. And you——

Ms. CONLEY.—force.

Senator INHOFE.—you agree with him.

Ms. CONLEY. I do agree with him. And I think yesterday's display of the cruise missiles reinforces exactly what General Dunford was saying.

Senator INHOFE. Do you agree, General Jones?

General JONES. I do agree with that.

Senator INHOFE. Let me tell you a concern that I had. This was in yesterday's Politico. It was talking about—Captain Jeff Davis told reporters the United States has a good awareness about the skies over—has begun routing—rerouting its airstrikes so they'll pass clear of the Russians. He said that we have taken some actions to ensure the safe separation of aircraft.

I look at that, that they are dictating what we're doing with our aircraft in making those determinations while we're sitting back and doing what is the most effective way to respond to them. Do you—am I wrong?

General KEANE. Well, it certainly appears that way. And, listen, we have full visibility of the airspace and also these airfields that are in Syria. We have very sophisticated radars for this purpose. Actually, a little bit better than the Russians. And we can actually track an airplane taking off from any airfield in Syria, and follow that airplane. So, we have positive control, in the sense of where are the Russian airplanes and what are—where are our airplanes? So, the idea that, to avoid some kind of air conflict, that we would stop or curtail our operations against ISIS, which we've said we were going to defeat, makes no sense to me.

Senator INHOFE. Have you ever seen this in your long career in the military before? Of us responding——

General KEANE. No, I have not. I can't recall anything like it.

Senator INHOFE. Yeah.

Just briefly on the Ukraine situation, do you think that this lull that we're experiencing right now might be due to the fact that they are—as we've pointed out, the military is strong, but they're in a weakened position, financially, economically, that maybe they can't—they're not able to do it? And the reason I'm asking that— I was over there when they had their parliamentary elections, and they—for the first time in 96 years, there's not one Communist in their Parliament. And I think that's very significant, and I would look for him to stop the lull and get back in. Do you think that the lull is going to last a while? Or do you think——

General KEANE. You're talking about in Russian military modernization?

Senator INHOFE. Uh-huh.

General KEANE. Yeah.

Senator INHOFE. No. No, I'm talking about what's happening right now with the aggressive nature of Putin in the Ukraine. It's slowed down a little bit now. Do you think that it's because they don't——

General KEANE. Yes. I—my sense of it is, that is just a pause.

Senator INHOFE. Yeah.

General KEANE. You know, politically, I believe he achieved what he wanted, and that is this government that was anti-Russian, to a sense, has turned its head away from the thought that it would be economically integrated into Europe or militarily integrated. He sort of—he has accomplished that. But, the fact that he's building those two bases there, Senator, tells you that he has not given up on——

Senator INHOFE. Yeah

General KEANE.—more activity in eastern Ukraine.

Senator INHOFE. Yeah. Yeah.

44

Lastly, the—you made the comment, Ms. Conley, that—and, as you know, we—as all of you know, we just passed our defense authorization bill. There's been a veto threat on parts of this. And this very much concerns us. You had said something to—during your statement. I don't think it was in your public—your published statement. But, you said you are very supportive of what we're trying to do with the National Defense Authorization Act (NDAA). Would you be specific as to what is really in there that you approve of and that you are enthusiastic about?

Ms. CONLEY. Thank you, Senator.

And, just to your previous question, I think Mr. Putin is dialing it down in Ukraine because he would like the European Union to lift sanctions, and they have to make that decision in the next couple of months. So, I think he's trying to reduce that——

Senator INHOFE. NDAA.

Ms. CONLEY. On the NDAA, specifically, there is an amendment that speaks about looking at the Arctic and seeing the strategic picture of the Arctic, assessing and making those assessments of what the capability gaps are. I think it is time—we have studied this issue, and there are pile and piles of studies, but we now have to look at this region more strategically. And within the NDAA, there is a specific discussion about how to look at the Arctic. I think it's also—in the NDAA, there's also discussion about Poland and east—and looking at increasing our force posture. These are exactly the strong signals that we need to send, and I thank the committee for their thoughtfulness on trying to get at this problem.

Senator INHOFE. Yeah, well, it's—help us get it through.

Thank you.

Senator MCCAIN. Senator King.

Senator KING. Thank you, to the panel. This has been very thought-provoking and very helpful.

I do—I share your concerns about the Arctic and what's going on there strategically. I'm going to defer to my colleague from Alaska, who I—will—am quite confident will discuss that issue in some detail.

Senator SULLIVAN. You're correct.

[Laughter.]

Senator KING. I've—yeah, I'm a mindreader. I don't——

Let's talk about Syria for a minute. It seems to me, if you boil it down to its most essential element, Putin wants Assad in more than we want him out. He's willing to make a commitment that we haven't been willing to make over the past 2 or 3 years. Our policy has been a—benign neglect is too strong a term, but it's been a kind of—go slow, hope that momentum would eventually push him out. And apparently there was some progress being made this summer, and Putin decided he was going to reverse that. And we're faced with a decision of, How important is it for us to get rid of Assad? And is it worth risking a war?

I have this historical dilemma of whether this is the Sudetenland of 1938 or Sarajevo in 1914. I'm not sure it's worth starting World War III over Assad. The Archduke is long forgotten, and, at some point, Assad will be, as well. But, that's the strategic dilemma, is, What is our real interest?

Now, I do think—and, General Keane, you mentioned—I think it was very significant—that Russia does have a legitimate serious fear about ISIL and about Islamic jihadism. Perhaps that's an opportunity for us to make common cause with them, just as we did on the chemical weapons issue. And countries ultimately only act in their own interest. And this is a place where we do have a coincidence of interest, and perhaps that's an area that we can focus upon, separate from the issue of Assad.

Finally, Ms. Conley, I was fascinated by your discussion of Iron Curtain 2.0. It seems to me what we're talking about here today is Containment 2.0. We're talking about a strategy of, What do we do with Russia? Is it expansionist or is it—is this historic Russian paranoia, going back to Napoleon and Hitler, and feelings of threat from the West? Are they trying to build a defensive perimeter, or are they—do they want to ultimately control France and England and the United States? How do you—what is it they want?

General JONES. I'll take a stab at that. The—I think, deep in the—as I mentioned in my remarks, deep in Mr. Putin's thought process is, he wants to correct what he sees as a—an injustice with regard to the—how the Cold War ended. He wants his borders and——

Senator KING. But, does that mean he wants to take control of——

General JONES. No.

Senator KING.—Poland again, for example?

General JONES. No. But, I think that it does mean that he will push his borders away from Russia. He wants a—he wants peripheral states, as much as possible. And he's consumed—I honestly believe he's consumed by this idea that we are his natural enemies. I mean, he—he is the type—he—I define his leadership as a negative type of leadership, in the sense that people like him need an enemy to make themselves look good. And it's like the——

Senator KING. Well, clearly that's what he's doing politically.

General JONES. Exactly. And——

Senator KING. Take the people's mind off the lousy Russian——

General JONES. Exactly.

Senator KING.—economy.

General JONES. So—but, he's been successful, because we—he's moving faster than we can act, than we've acted. NATO, General Breedlove, has done some very innovative things, within certain constraints that he faces, in terms of the organization and how NATO makes decisions. But, I think Mr. Putin will pay attention when he sees decisive action. Now, what form that's going to take, we're going to have to wait and see. But, he's—I—he's going to continue to do this—to exhibit this kind of behavior until he's confronted with a——

Senator KING. I've always thought of Russian foreign policy as like a thief in a hotel that tries every door until he finds one that's open. And, as long as their doors are closed, as long as NATO exists and is vigorous and represents a line, that's the policy that I think you're recommending.

General JONES. Exactly. But, he has not seen that yet, so until we demonstrate that—and American leadership is absolutely essential in creating the conditions that will show that all doors are securely locked and that he can't——

Senator KING. But, I think it's awfully important, as you pointed out, the first—it was interesting, your first point was economic.

General JONES. Exactly.

Senator KING. That was what ultimately brought about the decline of the Soviet Union, and that also is what can undermine this new expansion.

General JONES. Exactly.

Ms. CONLEY. Senator King, I think every great power must have a sphere of influence, and Mr. Putin is doing it by force.

Regarding NATO, he would seek to undermine—if he can put a—you know, just a—run a train through NATO credibility, that's the best thing he could do. He wants NATO to collapse. How do you get to a new bargain is if—you know, the Warsaw Pact disintegrated, NATO survived. The only way you get to a new European security architecture, and the only way you get this grand bargain, where, ''This is yours and I'll let you keep that,'' is, you have to undermine the credibility of the NATO alliance. So, if he can divide the alliance, if he can put—if he can provoke a government for taking actions that other NATO allies won't support because—sort of the Georgia scenario—you provoke until there's an action, and then you blame the victim for doing that. That's the Ukraine scenario, as well. This divides the alliance. He believes that there's a civilizational challenge here, that the great Russian civilization has to fight against the decadence of the West.

And so, there is a slight ideological component to this, so it's not about invading Poland. It's so eroding America and NATO's credibility that it just sort of dissolves on its own. And therefore, Russia can exert its own influence and its own power, and it's demonstrating that it, in itself, is a superior model of development.

General KEANE. You know, piling onto that, I totally agree. This is not the occupation of his strategic buffer on his border. The burden of that, you know, is something that he doesn't want. This is about fragmenting the NATO alliance. I clearly think it's a strategic issue for them. I think they're going to probe to see how they can best do that, politically and militarily. They already know that Portugal, Spain, and Canadians are doubtful participants. I think they're going to—they will use the Baltics, likely as the best vehicle because of the Russian minority population there. You have—you've got to believe there's people like Jim and myself that are sitting around Putin and throwing the question on the table, ''Will Angela Merkel really respond to an incursion in the Baltics with the little green men and put her infantry in there to thrust them out?'' I mean, that's—I don't know the answer to that. And just the fact that that question is there gives them some leverage. So, I think that's what this is really about.

The second thing, in reference to, How could we cooperate with Russia?—I thought we had a lost opportunity, post-9/11, because of Russia's experience with radical Islam. Putin was the first guy that called the President of the United States, you know, based on what happened here. And this is someplace where we could truly work to cooperate. They have huge experience with radical Islam. They obviously have great concerns about it. We've been involved in it now for 15 years ourselves. We actually were involved in it years before that, but we never responded.

So, this is an area where I believe we need a global alliance to deal with it, and I think this is an area where the United States and Russia could exercise some leadership together to put together that alliance.

Senator KING. And I believe Russia is prepared to do that. At least they've indicated over the summer that they are.

Thank you very much.

Thank you, Mr. Chairman.

Senator MCCAIN. Ambassador, do you want to chime in here? You——

Ambassador SESTANOVICH. Let me just add one thing to this picture of Putin's view of Europe, because I do think he imagines that he can, with a combination of assets, be the dominant power in Europe, because, above all, Europe is divided, unable to act in a way that just—he has expressed his contempt for. But, I don't think we should underestimate the lessons that he's learned over the past couple of years. He has been surprised by the way in which the United States and Europe have responded to the Ukraine crisis. He expected this to go much more easily for him. And it has been a chastening experience.

Senator MCCAIN. Wow. I don't think the Ukrainians believe that.

Senator Wicker.

Senator WICKER. General Keane, to what extent did this surprise action by Russia in Syria represent an intelligence failure?

General KEANE. Well, I don't know, myself, what we do know and what the President has been told. Just seeing the reaction, certainly, of the National Command Authority, it appears, by every indication, that, you know, we didn't have much forewarning of this, you know, other than when he started to deceptively bring his airplanes in. You know, he flew his fighters in underneath his large cargo aircraft so they wouldn't be picked up on radar, and then he was—it was obvious that he was constructing something at the base. I think the first signs that I believe we knew something were physical signs that something was changing at the airbase. I don't know that for a fact, because I'm not privileged to have those classified briefings anymore.

Senator WICKER. Not—General Jones, it's not comforting about our intelligence capability there, is it?

General JONES. I think we were surprised by that.

Senator WICKER. Thank you very much.

Let me say that, as outrageous as Mr. Putin's actions have been in Syria, there's one thing you can say for him. He's standing by his only friend in the region. And so, let me ask you this, General Keane. To the extent that Mr. Putin and the people around him are looking at the Baltic states, what signals are they looking for about the decisions this administration is about to make with regard to Afghanistan? And what will that say about our resolve to stand by people who've taken our side in very important areas of the world?

General KEANE. Yeah. That's a great question. I think this is one of Putin's major points that he's making strategically, is that he's—he will stand by his friends and his allies, and he's willing to put muscle to that to accomplish that. And I think—I suspect Putin was somewhat in disbelief to watch America abandon Mubarak in Egypt, to watch America abandon Iraq, to watch America retreat from Yemen, and to watch America retreat from Libya. And he has a different playbook entirely from that. And here comes Afghanistan, as you just mentioned. I think we're going to make this decision: a force level that will not be that effective in helping to maintain security and stability in Afghanistan and will further put the country at risk. That will be read by Putin as another sign of America arbitrarily making decisions about the conditions of a war zone and, because we no longer want to be in it, moving away from it despite those conditions. Certainly, our allies have all seen this track record of retreat and withdrawal, and obviously it has to give them concerns.

You know as well as I do that anybody that talks to people in the Middle East region—there is not a country in the Middle East who we have a relationship with who has—who doesn't have doubts about America, in terms of its reliability and its trustworthiness to back them up in times of peril. That is a fact, and it's indisputable. I haven't talked to a Baltic leader, but I'm certain they have some issues with it. I also know, though, that they truly appreciate the forward positioning of troops and airpower in their country, because that is a positive sign.

Senator WICKER. General Jones, those are pretty strong words by General Keane. Would you care to follow up on those?

General JONES. I don't think there's any doubt that, in the areas that we deal with, particularly in the Middle East, that our reliability factor has suffered a serious blow over the last few years. Wasn't intended that way. I—you know, I thought that the announcement of a pivot towards Asia was a mistake to announce it that way, because when you pivot toward something, you're pivoting away from something, and the Arabs took it quite differently than what, perhaps, we intended.

Senator WICKER. You know, I don't remember being a part of that decision as a Member of Congress for the last 21 years.

Let me see if I can sneak a question in for Ms. Conley. It seems to me, as an advocate—as a strong advocate of Radio Free Europe and Radio Liberty, that the Russians have been eating our lunch lately when it comes to the information war. How important is this? And do you agree with my assessment?

Ms. CONLEY. Senator, I fully agree with your assessment. Unfortunately, the tools that were successful during the Cold War—Radio Free Europe, Voice of America—are no longer the tools that are going to be able to penetrate an incredibly and sophisticated strategic communications campaign. I was in Bulgaria, 3 weeks ago, where Russian oligarchs and firms have basically purchased every media outlet in Bulgaria. There is no ability to penetrate that. And they're not listening to Voice of America. When you go into eastern Estonia, to Narva, they are only listening to Russian media, and they're given a completely different universe that they're living in. We have seen the efficiency of Russian trolls and tweeting incorrect information that's happening in the United States that can, you know, cause concern. We are not able, at this moment, to counter this campaign, but we need to employ a much more effective strategy.

I don't know if it's government propaganda, but I think it's a very sophisticated plan that works with social media outlets, those that are still open in Russia, although they're very few, and they're blocked repeatedly. But, we must work much harder at focusing on European public opinion, which is quite negative, as well as in Russia.

But, this is the great challenge of our time, and we really don't have an effective answer.

Senator WICKER. Thank you.

Senator MCCAIN. Senator Cotton.

Senator COTTON. Thank you.

I want to return to a point that General Keane was discussing earlier. The Pentagon confirmed, yesterday, that American pilots are now being told to alter their routes to get out of the way of Russian aircraft. In your long career, you said you can't recall a time in which that's happened. Does that apply to the entire military? Can you recall a time in which any American troop has ever been told to change his action to avoid an enemy?

General KEANE. I don't have a direct reference for it. There probably is something along those lines, but I don't—in modern warfare, since the United States has had global responsibility, I don't have a reference for it.

Senator COTTON. General Jones, you have a long and distinguished career, as well. Can you recall a time in which—told American troops to avoid an enemy?

General JONES. No.

Senator COTTON. I certainly haven't served as long as you two have, but I can't recall receiving or giving such an order, either. America doesn't avoid our enemies.

General Keane, you also said that Vladimir Putin is no dummy. He recalls the experience of Afghanistan when they lost thousands of lives and it made the Soviet leadership very unpopular with the Russian people. The key part of—one key part of Afghanistan was United States active intervention in providing billions of dollars worth of weapons and support to various Afghan fighting forces. Is that correct?

General KEANE. Yes, most definitely.

Senator COTTON. Is there any reason to think that Vladimir Putin is going to repeat the experience in Syria that the Soviet Union had in Afghanistan if there's not that kind of peer competitor there to help check through active intervention?

General KEANE. The—in reference to what—what actions are you speaking to that he would take?

Senator COTTON. I am actually speaking of U.S. actions. We all know what Ronald Reagan did in Afghanistan in the Cold War. Is Vladimir Putin apt to face the same kind of quagmire that Soviets faced in Afghanistan in the—given the complete lack of action of the United States in Syria?

General KEANE. Yeah, right. The—clearly, what we have done in Syria, one, on the side to support the opposition forces, in my judgment, from the beginning, has been totally and completely inadequate. And we have had very competent people on President Obama's national security team that were advocating a much more robust strategy, as far back as 2012. Others advocating it before that. And the administration has never moved. What they did move is covertly dealing with the Central Intelligence Agency (CIA)-trained force to provide them with some weapons capability. But, that is not sufficient, and we—despite all of that—think of this—despite all of that, because of the weaknesses of the Syrian regime—that army's down to about 120,000 from 220-plus, desertions, broken equipment, using one or two aircraft a day—one or two aircraft a month, morale low, many of the conscripts that they should be bringing into the service are the young men that are fleeing into Europe as part of the refugees—so, there's real problems there. Despite our faulty programs, the opposition forces, to include the al-Qaeda, have been able to put this regime still in jeopardy for the second time. And, unfortunately, what's going to take place now, I think, is, Putin is going to be successful in supporting the Syrian—to push back on many of these gains. And I don't think we're going to do anything more than what we are doing to help the opposition forces. Those decisions have been made. I don't believe the President's going to take any action, you know, to protect them, which he could, by establishing free zones for them, and certainly some other actions that he could take to protect them, as I mentioned in my statement.

So, I think we are where we are, in terms of U.S. support. And, as it pertains to the rest of Syria, we don't have a strategy to defeat ISIS in Syria. It doesn't exist.

Senator COTTON. I, regrettably, agree about our policy in Syria.

Ambassador Sestanovich, in your statement, point five, you say that, ''We should all worry about where Russia's reckless behavior will lead next. Most of us have been wrong in anticipating Russian actions in the past couple of years.'' I would agree with that, as well. So, I would have a question for the panel about the future, given what General Keane just said.

My son has reached the age at which we play a game commonly known as ''Peek-a-boo.'' In my household, I refer to it as ''Surprised-by-Putin.'' It's amusing when a 5-month-old is repeatedly surprised by the same action over and over again in close succession. It's very dangerous when a President is. So, what's the next surprise that Vladimir Putin is going to spring on the United States in the West?

Ambassador SESTANOVICH. Tough question, Senator.

I think we may discover, as some of the other panelists have said, that there's another round of Russian policy in Ukraine. I think right now they're unsure of how to handle this crisis, but they have not written off their investment there. I would certainly pay attention to that.

If you ask about crises in the Middle East emanating from Syria, you know, I'd look to the spillover to other countries that have been very worried about what is going to happen and have not gotten a lot of help from us. The fact that Turkish airspace was violated over the weekend is a warning by the Russians, but it's not the only way in which this could spill over. Syria, unfortunately, has got a lot of neighbors in the Middle East, and Russian policy is going to prolong this civil war.

I'd just put one little extra piece on the board for you to look at if you have General Keane's maps in front of you. One country that is not on the map here is Azerbaijan. Azerbaijan is the country off whose coast the Russians fired those cruise missiles. It's been able to sustain its independence over a long period of time, but it's in play. It's not the only—it's not the biggest prize here. It's not the—it's not likely to be sucked into the war. But, the Russians move on a lot of different fronts, and their aim is, as many of the panelists have said, to restore influence over other countries of the former Soviet Union. Watch that space.

Senator McCain. Senator Ayotte.

Senator Ayotte. Thank you, Chairman.

I want to thank all of you for being here today.

General Keane, you said that aggression unanswered, you fear, leads to more aggression.

And, General Jones, I believe you talked about how we need to increase our NATO presence in eastern Europe, among many of the things that you discussed, and that there's a greater risk by not increasing U.S.-NATO presence, versus those who want to say, "Let's not incite Russia." If you look at what we—what has happened without us, I guess, doing anything to incite Russia, it's been pretty astounding.

So, with the tremendous military experience between both of you—General Keane, General Jones—I mean, it's incredible what you've done for the country—I wanted to ask you—if we stay the course, if we stay where we are, which is, as I see it, really no response, that we are letting them kind of take their course as to what they're doing both in Ukraine, where, yes, we have economic sanctions, but we certainly haven't provided any military support for the Ukrainians—if we don't increase NATO presence, if we don't take some actions and we let Russia pretty much own the airspace in these areas, what do you think—what is the thing that worries you most and keeps you up at night, that if we stay the course of where we are now, which seems to be letting the Russians take whatever action they want to take at any time?

General Jones. I think it's possibly the beginning of the end of the North Atlantic Treaty Organization. I think it's that serious. We just can't sit back and let this happen.

In 2004 or 2005, we started withdrawing a lot of our forces from Europe. Some of us had some serious discussions with the then-Secretary of Defense about the tradeoff of doing that. Our belief, when I was in Europe, was that, yes, you could reduce some of the infrastructure and some of the forces, but it should be balanced by rotational forces elsewhere in eastern Europe, particularly in Bulgaria and Romania, where we—where those countries helped build bases that would accommodate rotational forces, and then, because of the demands on our troop strengths in Iraq and Afghanistan, they were never really used. Happily, now we are starting to see those bases being used. And I would strongly suggest that—you know, the old adage "a virtual presence is actual absence" is absolutely correct. And we need to bolster our presence, and NATO needs to show itself as an alliance of 28 countries that really adheres to what it says and what it's for. And it should become more proactive as a way of dissuading other engagements. Sitting back and being reactive and then debating it for 6 months, hoping for

100-percent consensus among 28 countries, is not a formula for success with Vladimir Putin.

Senator AYOTTE. General Keane?

General KEANE. Yes. Clearly, the United States has been the dominant country in the Middle East that's outside the region—our own self-interests, obviously—economic, stability and security of the region. And we've been willing to take action to ensure that stability and security.

Enter Russia. Russia, with this alliance with Iran, cannot be understated, in terms of its strategic significance. It's going to have profound impact on the region. Every country in the region will be impacted by it and will be making adjustments to the new geopolitical landscape that Iran and Russia are creating for us. These are allies of ours that are being impacted by it. Why? Because of their concern about their strategic enemy: Iran. And, as a result of that, they have to leverage their relationship with Russia. So, our influence—listen, we're still a major player in the Middle East. I'm not suggesting we're not. But, I am suggesting we have diminished, in the last number of years. And with this alliance, this will be an accelerant to actually reduce our influence more considerably. So, that's number one.

Number—you're going to make a comment?

Senator AYOTTE. Well, I actually also wanted you to speak—in the context of this alliance between Iran and Russia, how does this deal play into it? Does it play into it at all?

General KEANE. Well, obviously Russia supported the deal as much as the United States did. They saw it in their interest to do so. Certainly, Iran's behavior for the last 35 years should have been on the table as a condition for the deal, but it was removed.

The other thing—I totally agree with General Jones—I think, strategically, it—the objective in Europe is the NATO alliance. And I think we're likely to see its unraveling, to be frank about it. Have you seen these surveys that they published about European countries, their willingness to defend themselves, and a majority of the people are unwilling to do that? What does that tell you? Much less collectively come to the aid of another country that is burdened by Russian aggression. The—strategically, he will break that alliance, and he's not going to have to take much military action to do it, in my judgment. And that is going to be a tragedy.

This requires U.S. leadership. And I think Jim laid out some careful points that we could exercise strategically, but we have to lead, and we have to have the resolve to do that.

General JONES. Could I just piggyback on that?

I just want to emphasize the fact that, although we're talking about NATO as a military alliance, there is a military component to what we can do to restore NATO, but the economic strategy is also very important, and the political strategy. So, I think it's three things that have to come together to have a—an effective strategy to deal with the—Mr. Putin's Russia as it is today.

Senator AYOTTE. Thank you.

Senator MCCAIN. Senator Donnelly.

Senator DONNELLY. Thank you, Mr. Chairman.

And thanks, to all the witnesses.

General Keane, I'd like to ask you this, first, but, you know, throw it open to everybody. So, we lead, and we put in no-fly zones, and we tell them, "End the barrel bombs," and that, "If you do, we'll crater the runways." What do you think Putin's response will be? And it's—you know, there's obviously no guarantees, but, you know, How do you think that will—where do you think he goes then?

General KEANE. I don't know. He has a range of options. Obviously, he can escalate right along with us if he chooses to. But, I think it's that. It—when you focus on that, in terms of "What is his escalation response?"—is the thing that paralyzed us from taking action. I mean, I think—I do believe there's prudent things, you know, that can be done.

Senator DONNELLY. Do those seem—they seem like prudent—you know, we've been talking about a no-fly zone for a while here, ending the barrel bombs, which the Chairman has talked about repeatedly. Those seem like prudent steps to take, to me.

General KEANE. Yeah, they're not easy, though, and let's——

Senator DONNELLY. Right.

General KEANE. Let me tell you why. Obviously, with Putin's airpower there, and enforcing a no-fly/no-bomb zone is more challenging now. In the south, it—and to enforce a no-fly zone, you actually have to have someone on the ground to also protect that zone from infiltration from the regime or, actually, Jabhat al-Nusra. So, in the south, we can put together a—I prefer to call it a free zone, where the moderates would be protected there, and we would be able to bring refugees in as a sanctuary. And the reason for that is, we have an effective ground force there in the Free Syrian Army. In the north, where we truly want to do it, and where the Turks have interest in it as well, it's much more challenging. And this is the reason. We don't have the density of moderate forces there that we have in the south. And Jabhat al-Nusra would likely infiltrate it or overtly attack it.

Senator DONNELLY. Well, maybe a better term on my part would have been a safe zone, where they don't get barrel-bombed from the sky, where things like that——

General KEANE. Well, that's what I call a free zone. But, we—the south, I think we can achieve it. In the north, it's challenging, and I'm not confident that we would have the same results. And it certainly risks escalation.

Senator DONNELLY. Do you—I'm sorry.

Ambassador SESTANOVICH. I'll give you a—I'll give you a firmer answer, actually, than General Keane. I think if you get—if you have—if you convey that the United States and its allies in the region are going to take serious military action, you will get a serious Russian diplomatic response. That is, for the first time, Putin will start saying, "You know, we need to talk about the future of the Syrian regime" in a way that has not been true until now. I think the Russians have not felt that they have to take seriously what we say about the future of Syria, because we're not playing.

If you want to play in this game, you have to be prepared to put some assets on the table. And I don't think we can expect to affect the political equation until the Russians think that there's a—that the military risks to them are greater than they calculate.

Senator DONNELLY. And do you think if there is that pushback and then you combine it with time and you combine it with $40-a-barrel oil, is there a window for Putin to be doing these things where in—2 years from now, if we push back during that time, and hold firm, that, at some point, he just says, "Enough," you know, "We'll try to cooperate and get this done together?" Because at some point he looks at—do you think he sees financial difficulties down the road for him, as well?

General?

General KEANE. Oh, yes, absolutely. I mean, his financial reserves are depleting rather dramatically. If the economy stays the way it is, certainly that's going to have some—you know, some impact on him. But, I still believe that Putin's view is much larger than just a couple of years, in terms of what he portends, strategically, for himself.

But, let me just add to your other point. If we establish free zones, you know, for moderate opposition forces, but also sanctuaries for refugees, that gets world-opinion support rather dramatically. If Putin is going to attack that, then world opinion is definitely against him. You take this issue right off the table, in terms of why he's in Syria. And if you're doing that, and contributing to the migration that's taken place by your aggressive military actions, then world opinion will have some rather, I think, significant impact on him.

General JONES. If I could, it's—we have a model in 1991 in Iraq, where we not only partitioned the north and the south, but we cratered the runways, we were able to get Saddam's air force completely grounded. But, what we also did was, by creating those zones, particularly in the north, we avoided a significant refugee problem. And I think that a mistake was made, back on the redline days, when we didn't do that as a response to his using chemical weapons. I believe that Europe would not have been suffering the refugee problem that they have now, and I think—I completely agree with General Keane that, if you tie it to the safety of—and security of innocent civilians, and you take—make it a big enough chunk in the country—I think that that is a powerful argument to do that. And I agree that it's harder in the north and that that's something we should look at in the south.

Senator DONNELLY. Thank you, Mr. Chairman.

Senator McCAIN. Both—you agree, Ms. Conley and Ambassador, with that assessment?

Ambassador SESTANOVICH. I certainly do. And I think you'd see some impact in Putin's behavior sooner than 2 years from now. Putin doesn't fold his tent lightly, and he's not going to admit quickly that this entire operation has been a fiasco for him. But, if there's pushback, he will not necessarily just continue plunging forward.

Senator DONNELLY. Wasn't thinking that he'd wait 2 years, but, in his mind, at all points, you'd have to think is, "What's my currency balance at the moment?" as well.

Senator McCAIN. Ms. Conley?

Ms. CONLEY. Well, in many ways, though, a lot of this adventurism is because the domestic situation is continuing to deteriorate. Russian inflation is very high. He's having to tell the oligarchs that they can't quite get as much funding. And they're in desperate straits. The sanctions and the low energy prices have had impact.

But, remember, he's created the national narrative that he's—Russia is encircled by enemies. And he controls the media space, and he's created a warlike environment. So, I think there's probably a little more longevity here, even if the economic situation continues to fundamentally deteriorate. I think his vulnerability, as we saw in Ukraine, is casualties. So, if you do make the military cost higher, that he can't cover up—and they've done a masterful job of suppressing—even the mothers of Russian soldiers are now foreign agents because they were talking about the disappearance of their sons in Ukraine. That is a vulnerability. But, his control over his media space is—so, this can go on for a long time. But, we can make the calculation—the risk higher for him. And I think, if he does run into strength, he responds to that strength and adjusts.

I recall—and, Senator McCain, you know this much better. This was during the Russia-Georgian conflict when we had to fly back—Georgian soldiers back to Georgia. And, you know, a C–5A coming in, and it's, you know, ''Don't do this.'' And we said, ''Get out of our way.'' And they responded to that. But, we have to be very strong in what we're going to do. And I know you remember those days very well.

Senator McCain. Senator Ernst.

Senator Ernst. Thank you, Mr. Chair.

Thank you, Ms. Conley and gentlemen, for being here today, and your service to our country.

For General Jones and General Keane, last week I had voiced my concerns regarding the new intelligence-sharing agreement between Iraq, Russia, Iran, and Assad's Syria. And, like all events in Iraq, it seems, according to Deputy Secretary of Defense Robert Work, this agreement caught the administration by surprise. You know, hello. However, I'm not surprised, considering the Iranian influence in Iraq seems to have really eclipsed our own as the Iraqi government continues on its trajectory towards a very sectarian, noninclusive government and our administration has a lack of decisiveness in that region when it comes to fighting ISIS.

So, considering the efforts of all of our men and women in uniform and the billions of American taxpayer dollars that have been put into Iraq, supporting the Iraqi people and the Iraqi government, I am troubled that the Iraqi government has entered into this information-sharing agreement. And they did this without consultation to the United States. So, I do think this puts our intelligence professionals at risk, and our country at a greater risk.

And so, if you could maybe talk a little bit about what those risks might be to the American public and why we should or should not have—or why they should or should have not entered into this information-sharing agreement.

General Keane. Well, Congresswoman—I mean, Senator, thank you, and thank you for your military service——

Senator Ernst. Thank you.

General Keane.—and your leadership.

You know, the—when you think about Iraq, we not only lack sufficient resources in trying to assist the indigenous forces there, I also think, politically, we're not doing nearly what we should have been doing, because you cannot have success in Iraq without Sunni participation——

Senator ERNST. Right.

General KEANE.—in a significant way. And it has cost Maliki's ineptness and—the nefarious character that he is, that excluded the Sunnis politically from participation. And I know everybody knows this answer, but what are we doing to assist that? You know, one of the things we—one of the things we've been advocating is, we need a three-star military headquarters there, with the Ambassador, that interacts routinely with Prime Minister Abadi for political reasons, as well as military reasons, similar to way Ryan Crocker and General Dave Petraeus did with Maliki before. And it's not something to be taken lightly, because it is the political decision to include the Sunnis that becomes the lynchpin for success of the indigenous force. You're never going to be able to succeed until their participation is there. You can actually clear Ramadi. Let's assume we clear Ramadi next week with predominant Shi'a militia forces and some degree of Iraqi army. What is going to keep ISIS out of Ramadi is Sunnis, Sunnis who are armed and trained and have the resolve to stay there, just as it will be in Mosul.

Senator ERNST. So, General——

General KEANE. That participation is totally dependent on a political inclusion of the Sunnis. So, the fact that Abadi is making this deal—and I think it portends a statement he's not making publicly, that the United States is not supporting him in a way that he needs, and the Iranians are, the Russians will be, and I think he's making a shift, right before our eyes, without making any public pronouncements about his loss of confidence in the United States.

Senator ERNST. So, General Keane, basically the lack of diplomatic participation by our administration, as well as militarily, has led to this information-sharing agreement, would you agree?

General KEANE. I think it has. I mean, Prime Minister Abadi came to this country for his first visit with the President of the United States, and he left, essentially, with nothing more than what he already had. And that was his first visit. He had a shopping list of what he wanted. Four weeks later, he's in Moscow, and he's cutting an arms deal with Russia. The deal has already been done. Now, he doesn't want to buy Russian stuff, he wants American equipment. He can't even get the American equipment on time in the numbers he wants for the deals he already has with the United States. That's how frustrated they are with just supporting him on the decisions we've already made, much less additional support.

So, if you're facing an enemy that's breathing down on your country and occupies one-third of your country, and you're challenged to retake that territory and evict them, and you're comforted by the fact that the United States is coming to your aid, but that aid is so shallow—you can understand what he's doing. He wants to protect the sovereignty of his country. And if he—if Iran's going to be the helper or if Russian's going to be the helper, he's probably going to take it.

Senator ERNST. He's going to take it.

And I'm sorry, I know I'm running out of time, but, General Jones, if you would comment, just very briefly. Do you believe that now with this intelligence agreement sharing arrangement that Iran and Russia will be able to exploit intelligence that we have had and gathered in Iraq?

General JONES. Oh, I think that deal is probably not in our best interest.

Senator ERNST. Okay, thank you. That's excellent. I appreciate it.

Thank you, Mr. Chair.

Senator MCCAIN. Senator Sessions.

Senator SESSIONS. Thank you.

This is really a valuable panel. We've got great witnesses, and have shared with us information about a very grave foreign policy time in our country. It's unbelievable that we're drifting without a kind of a strategy to seriously deal with Russia or the whole Middle East. Somehow I think a Nixon-Kissinger, we'd be in better shape today.

Ambassador Sestanovich, George Kennan has been mentioned. I see you're the George Kennan scholar. Do you think that it is appropriate for the United States at this time to see—to take action to establish a more long-term strategy for the Middle East that would extend over decades, not just reacting to one event after another, one that our allies around the world could join with us on?

Ambassador SESTANOVICH. I have the greatest respect for George Kennan, but, actually, at the time, he was trying to develop a strategy that would be good even for a couple of years. And if we had a strategy that was good for a couple of years, we'd be way ahead of where we are now. So, let's not think decades. Sometimes long-termism can be a trap. Let's try to think about how to get our act together in a way that does us some good in the——

Senator SESSIONS. What about——

Ambassador SESTANOVICH.—short and middle term.

But, let me——

Senator SESSIONS. But an——

Ambassador SESTANOVICH. I—but, if I could answer your——

Senator SESSIONS.—agreement to agree on——

Ambassador SESTANOVICH. Yeah. Look, the main thing that the Russians have always thought about us in relation to them is that we have allies and that they didn't, and that they are all by themselves. This, of course, feeds a lot of insecurity on their part, but it is a genuine advantage for us. That advantage is at risk of being lost. I mean, we can squander this huge asset. And so, I would suggest that the place to start in thinking about a strategy that will be effective over the next couple of years or the next couple of decades is how to leverage this advantage that we have built up over half a century. And it's not—for reasons that the generals have mentioned, not easy to do at this point, because there are a lot of doubts about our strategic good sense and our staying power. But, these are still assets that are latent and can be recovered if we are at all serious about it.

Senator SESSIONS. Well, General Jones, you were our Supreme Allied Commander in Europe. You were there for a long time. I visited you and value your judgment. But, are you positive we could face the end of NATO? A European official of great experience said the refugee crisis could—is the greatest threat to the EU since World War II. He was panicked. A person you could trust, a man of judgment.

Well, so we're in Estonia and they wanted more American troops. We had 160——-40, I believe, or—but, I don't know—a company, I believe. And so, I asked you all, Well, how much were they spending on their defense budget? Little Estonia, right up there next to the border. And, of course, they were sincerely saying they were going to get to 2 percent. Well, we're at 3.6. Germany's hardly over 1 percent of their defense. And you made that—General Jones, you mentioned the poll. That was stunning to me. I mean, I wondered—I asked the Estonians, ''Why doesn't—why don't Germany or France put a company in here? It would be less expensive for them than for us.'' It's their backyard. But, apparently, that—is it a——

So, I'm very frustrated about that. I think they're not carrying their share of the load. I think they need to do it. But, their lack of will is so palpable, it seems to me that, if we don't lead and don't step up, they're not going—they'll just try to negotiate their way and not take any real serious action.

I've gone a bit in circles. Do you have any thoughts about the problem of Europe's will and how we can help fix that? And is it hopeful?

General JONES. At the NATO summit in 2002, the 19 countries that made up NATO at that time agreed unanimously that 2 percent of their gross domestic product would be provided for national defense. That soon became a floor. And very few of them actually did that, despite the pledges.

Ongoing in NATO right now is a reaffirmation of the fact that we need that—everybody needs to chip in that 2 percent. And I— and some countries are actually doing better. But, the—to Ms. Conley's admonition that the next Warsaw summit, next year, is critical, in many respects, not only in what NATO stands for, what it does, how it does it, but how it's funded, and the commitments that NATO members make now, with 28, should be universally agreed to and should absolutely be supported.

But, I do believe that our engagement in this 21st century is— got to be different than the 20th century engagement. We cannot just have military responses alone anymore. If you don't tie in economic development, governance, and rule of law in a more comprehensive, whole-of—you know, whole-of-nations involvement, and you don't show people that there's a better future for them at the end of whatever conflict they're going through, you're going to lose them, and you're going to create refugees all over the world. And if you like what's happening in the Middle East right now, we're going to love what's going to happen in Africa in another 10 years, when Nigeria collapses or another big country goes under.

So, this is a very difficult, dangerous time, where weakness is not something that we should show, because people draw—people like Mr. Putin will draw the long—wrong conclusions.

Senator SESSIONS. Thank you.

Thank you, Senator McCain. And I appreciate the comments——

Senator MCCAIN. Senator——

Senator SESSIONS.—for a zone for people—refugees. I think that's got to be done.

Senator MCCAIN. Senator from the Arctic.

[Laughter.]

Senator SULLIVAN. Thank you, Mr. Chairman.

And I want to thank the panel, this really incredible experience here, but also great insights.

Ms. Conley, I want to thank you, particular, not only for your testimony, your outstanding work on the Arctic. As my friend from Maine said, I am going to focus on the Arctic here.

In terms of the—you mentioned the NDAA, and I appreciate you mentioning that, because, you know, what we are really reacting to, as a Congress, to get serious—that's a requirement for no plan, actually, for the Arctic—was our current Arctic strategy, which you may have seen. This is DOD product, 13 pages, half of them are pictures. Climate change is mentioned six times; Russia once, in a footnote. It's not a serious strategy. So, what we're trying to do is get serious and have the Department of Defense get serious on that. So, thank you for mentioning it.

Also, in your testimony, you know, I think it's—appreciate all the—you talked about the massive Russian military buildup, which also includes—you didn't mention it in your testimony—four new brigade combat teams (BCT), and, as you mentioned, a new brigade headquarters for the military—Russia—Arctic military—40 ice-breakers, and more to come; some of those are nuclear powered. We have two. One is broken. So——

But, in terms of the three military exercises you mentioned, they didn't get a lot of press in the United States. Do you view those as provocative, in terms of what the Russians were doing, Ms. Conley?

Ms. CONLEY. I view the last one, the March 2015, because it was a snap exercise at full combat readiness. We need to get the Russians back to the rules that the OSCE—of transparency, 45-day notification over a certain level—because this is where misunderstandings and accidents happen. So, that, to me, was provocative and unprovoked, although——

Senator SULLIVAN. And we were pretty unaware of that.

Ms. CONLEY. We certainly were unaware of that.

Senator SULLIVAN. Let me ask you—I'd like the panel to take a look at this map. It kind of goes through what you were talking about in your testimony. The red is the Russians and recent build-ups. If you look in the right-hand corner, though, of that map, there's two blue dots. Those are two U.S. brigade combat teams. They're the only Arctic-trained American warriors that we have in the Active Duty forces. One of them is the 425. It's a brigade combat team in the Army. It's the only airborne BCT in the entire Asia-Pacific or the Arctic. The Department of Defense wants to, essentially, shut that down.

So, the Russians are building up dramatically. We're not even—you know, there are some people saying, "Hey, we've got to stand

up. We can't be provocative.'' We're not even being provocative.
We're just folding, in terms of Arctic forces.

In light of what the Russians are doing and a theme of this hearing about signaling—we've signaled weakness, Putin exploits weakness, his appetite grows after each meal—what do you think Vladimir Putin would think of the United States removing its only airborne BCT Arctic capability and really cutting our Arctic forces in half?

Ms. CONLEY. I think, Senator, that they view them very similar to, as General Jones said, that they viewed our reductions in Europe. We are leaving. We are leaving the playing field. I agree with you completely. We do not have much of a U.S. security architecture in the Arctic, other than our missile defense at Fort Greely——

Senator SULLIVAN. Right. Do you think that he'll see this as more weakness and possibly look to exploit it in other ways?

Ms. CONLEY. Well, I mean, we have told the Russians that they are our partners in the Arctic, and that would be true in the case of the Arctic Council. But, on the military component, we have not fully addressed and understood the dramatic shifts over the last 12 to 24 months that have occurred——

Senator SULLIVAN. Yeah.

Ms. CONLEY.—in militarization——

Senator SULLIVAN. But, you think there's a—we need to relook at that, given what's happening.

Ms. CONLEY. Oh, absolutely. And I said—it's not just for the Arctic's sake, although important changes are happening. We have to look at this at a broader theater. And that's what the first military exercise signaled——

Senator SULLIVAN. Yeah.

Ms. CONLEY.—that they're integrating theaters. So, what happens in the Baltic Sea, the North Sea, the Barents Sea, and the Arctic—it's a continuation of operations. So, we have to look at it holistically, not only the land component, as you rightly note, but also I'm particularly concerned, and what our allies—our Norwegian and British allies are very concerned—is the maritime component. Senator King was—the North Atlantic is becoming a much more active——

Senator SULLIVAN. Yeah.

Ms. CONLEY.—theater in maritime, as well as air.

Senator SULLIVAN. Let me ask—for General Jones and General Keane—you know, I've had the opportunity to train a lot in cold weather at Bridgeport and up in Alaska. Can infantry troops, say, based at Camp Pendleton or based at Fort Benning, go to the Arctic, operate in the mountains in 30-below-zero, in extreme cold, extreme winter climate? Can they do that easily, or do they—do you need troops to be able to acclimatize to that?

General JONES. You need special training, and you need—but, to the bigger strategic point: Since 1945, the United States has recognized that if you're not present where you need to be present, and you're absent, you create a vacuum. And vacuums are usually filled by people that don't have the—don't share your same interests. And, you know, I used the term ''virtual presence is actual absence,'' but actual absence means you're creating vacuums. And the

United States, if it desires to be a globally significant power by the year 2050, needs to think about strategically what we're going to do to avoid increasing the number of vacuums that we're creating around the world.

Senator SULLIVAN. Thank you.

General Keane?

General KEANE. Yeah, Senator, thanks for your military service.

I spent 4 years in Alaska as a company commander, paratrooper, jumping all over the place, and, you know, on different glaciers, et cetera. It was quite an experience. Yes, I mean, it—the acclimatization, the special equipment, everything that you need to operate in minus-30, minus-40-degree temperatures routinely, the toughness of the soldiers themselves to operate in an environment like that, that's why we have forces there, for that very reason. Parachute forces have a strategic capability.

Senator SULLIVAN. Yeah.

General KEANE. And that's why they're a value to us, to this day. Because you can seize an airfield with them very quickly and then bring in a lot of other things to help them out.

But, what this—what is happening here—and I hope the other Senators understand—is, the budget control authority and sequestration is driving the force structure of the Army down to World War II—pre-World War II numbers. So, the force structure peaked in fighting in Iraq and Afghanistan at 570-, and we couldn't fight those wars at this numbers simultaneously. We actually had to do it sequentially. And that's lost on a lot of people. We're at 490-, going to 450-, and the budget control authority and sequestration will take the Army to 420-. I was with the Chief of Staff and his four-stars just the other day, dealing with this very subject. And the question was asked, Why are we doing this? And he has no choice but to take brigades out of his force structure because of what the budget control authority is doing to him. Now, he does have the choice which brigades. And there is an argument and a tradeoff that he's trying to make. This was done in conjunction with the Pacific theater commander and where he also wanted his forces, not just the Army. So, that is an issue.

But, let me just say that we have a Democratic President and a Republican House of Representatives and a Republican Senate. And both of these entities are underwriting sequestration and the decapping of military capabilities and putting this country at a greater security risk than it needs to. And we've got to stop it. I mean, we've got to stop this, and stop this freefall of military capability.

Senator SULLIVAN. Thank you, Mr.—Mr. Chairman, may I ask—indulge one final question? This is an important topic to me.

Strategically, do you think it's a mistake to be taking our only airborne BCT out of the Arctic, given what we—this panel has been discussing for the last 3 hours, in terms of a massive increase with regard to what Putin is doing and how we are getting rid of the only Arctic warriors we have? I'll just ask all the members. You can just say yes or no if you think it's a strategic mistake.

Ms. CONLEY. I think we have to retain the current assets that we have in theater and look at how we can best augment to be able to rapidly respond and deploy, if necessary.

Ambassador SESTANOVICH. General Keane is absolutely right about the budget.

Senator SULLIVAN. General Jones? General Keane?

General JONES. Sorry. I agree with that.

General KEANE. Yes.

Senator SULLIVAN. Thank you.

Thank you, Mr. Chair.

Senator REED [presiding]. Thank you.

Senator Hirono, on behalf of the Chairman, let me recognize you.

Senator HIRONO. Thank you very much.

And I thank all of the panel members.

General Keane, thank you for once again pointing out the importance of taking responsible action to eliminate sequester on both the defense and nondefense side. This committee, of all committees, I think, fully understands the negative impact of sequestration on our military.

General Keane, you had mentioned, in response to Senator Reed's question about whether or not—some of the suggested actions that you put into your testimony raises the issue of whether or not we ought to be having a debate on a new Authorized Use of Military Force. And I think you acknowledged that some of the suggestions probably would warrant that.

Do the other panel members also agree? And, if so, should we not be beginning the debate on a new AUMF with regard to Syria?

Anyone? Do you think we don't need a new AUMF?

General JONES. Yes.

Senator HIRONO. We should begin the debate now? We—okay. Because we haven't done that. And that may be one of the reasons that we are having such a difficult time, in terms of our strategy in Syria.

In the Financial Times op-ed last Sunday, Dr. Brzezinski stated that it is time for—and I'm quoting him—"strategic boldness," end quote, calling on the United States to persuade—to persuade—so far, persuasion hasn't worked very well—persuade Moscow to act with us in stabilizing Syria and encouraging engagement by China.

And I'd like to ask the panel members, you know, What are your thoughts on a cooperative role between the United States and Russia, realizing that Russia—Putin is no fool, as one of you said, that, I think, he is as concerned—he must have some concerns about potential for mission creep for them in Syria, and them getting bogged down. So, you know, what are the conditions that would foster a discussion about a cooperative—cooperation between the United States and Russia, and the potential role of China in seeking stability in the Middle East?

I ask any of the panel members to——

Ambassador SESTANOVICH. I did not know what Zbig Brzezinski meant in that piece about bringing in China, so you'll have to ask him. But, I think the answer to your question, more broadly, is an easy one. The United States is not going to be able to have any meaningful cooperative—or discussion with Russia about cooperation unless it has its own thought-out strategy and is willing to bring some assets to the discussion, and act on its own if it can't cooperate. The administration has been very interested in cooperating, but it has pursued this discussion as though you could get the Russians to cooperate with you as a substitute for American action. And I think that has been a strategic mistake. The only way to really get a serious discussion with the Russians is to begin by thinking through what matters to us and what we are prepared to do, and then telling them. And then you can have a conversation. But, to just think of cooperation as a substitute for any independent action is a loser.

Senator HIRONO. Do the other panelists agree with that assessment?

Ms. CONLEY. I would just say, I think that moment of trying to think cooperatively expired a long time ago. And, to agree with Ambassador Sestanovich, at this point, it's—we have no strategy at what we're clear about and willing to enforce. So, the strategic cooperation is whether we go along with Mr. Putin or whether we don't.

General JONES. I would agree that you have to—you—we have to take some action that clearly shows that—that establishes a motivation for President Putin to want to sit down and talk about it. But, I think that—I think there's been too much talk and not enough action on our side.

General KEANE. Yeah, I totally agree. You know, Mr. Brzezinski, in that article, also talked about retaliation against the regime, as you recall in the article, as a result of their attacking, you know, our surrogate forces. And certainly that's an innovative thought. I don't know what—the merits of that, in bringing China into it. I do know that contributing—that Putin understanding our resolve and our commitment, judged by our actions and not by our rhetoric, will make a difference, in terms of pushing him to more thoughtful diplomatic action. It has the opportunity to do that. It also has the risk that it will not result in that. And it could result in military escalation. But, if that is the only lever that we're concerned about, is military escalation, it leaves us with this—the emptiness of the status quo. And that's where we are.

Senator HIRONO. And when you say ''action,'' you're talking about military action. That's what all of you are——

General KEANE. Well, I think we should approach him with everything that we have, in terms of putting pressure on him, but I do think we're out of time, given the military aggression that he is using, and he's been using for a number of years now, that we have to push back on that.

Senator HIRONO. And——

Ambassador SESTANOVICH. I would just add one—to the question about whether it's only military action we're talking about. I think an effective strategy is going to have to be one that brings together other countries in the region. And that's a political process. Those other countries are going to want to know what we are prepared to do. But, to begin with, to—the first kind of cooperation that has to be established for us to have any credibility in conversation with the Russians is with our own friends.

Senator HIRONO. Thank you.

Senator REED. On behalf of the Chairman, Senator Tillis, please.

Senator TILLIS. Thank you, Senator Reed.

Ambassador Sestanovich, I had a discussion with a diplomat earlier this week who seemed to share the view that the Russian incursion is doomed to fail. But, I don't really understand that. They try to use, as a rationale behind that, as to some $200 billion in reserves that they have to spend. What they're doing right now, relatively speaking, seems to be low cost. We don't seem to be discussing other partners that are already active in Syria and in the way of Iran and an Iranian nuclear deal that promises to free up assets and to allow that economy to create currency that could become, in my opinion—I want to validate this—a very material part of what Russia ultimately does in Syria. What are your thoughts on that?

Ambassador SESTANOVICH. Well, I wouldn't say the main cost that President Putin faces is an economic one or—and when people say that he is about—doomed to fail, I assume what they really mean is that the civil war will actually become more intense and that the Assad regime will be short of the kind of intervention that Putin is surely hoping he doesn't have to launch—would be further weakened.

Senator TILLIS. With—I think, in terms of high confidence—in the chart up there—in terms of high-confidence strikes being almost four-to-one for opposition targets, versus ISIS targets, wouldn't that seem to suggest that they get that and they're going to do everything they can to stamp out the opposition to make it less likely that a credible civil war could break out?

Ambassador SESTANOVICH. Yeah, I think that it's possible that they will have some near-term advantages—I mean, successes.

Senator TILLIS. And, General Jones, do you have something to say on that?

General JONES. I—it's a little hard to predict, but I think, in the short term, you're going to see some tactical successes, but there'll be adjustments on the battlefield. I'm unconvinced that the victory through airpower alone is going to achieve success in either Syria or Iraq.

General KEANE. The other dimension here is, you cannot underestimate the resolve of the Syrian people, in terms of what has happened to them these last 4 years, and their determination. When you think about it, they went up against a military machine that has all modern weapons, and they stood up against it with very little weaponry themselves. I mean, what has kept this in their fight is their absolute determination and will to change their country so that their families and communities can have a better life. And they're willing to die for it. And that resolve is still there. So, that is not going away. They will be able to push back. But, the civil war is not going away.

Senator TILLIS. And, to both General Keane and General Jones, I had another discussion with a diplomat who said that the White House's passive posture was not really what they wanted, that they're acting on the recommendations of the folks in the Pentagon. Does that seem credible to you, given where you are? Do you believe that the strategy that we have, which—erasing red lines and taking a passive position in a number of areas around the globe where we should be probably showing a little bit more assertion— does that seem logical that that would be the recommendations out of the Pentagon to the President?

General KEANE. Well, first of all—Jim and I are very familiar with this—the Pentagon does not make policy. National Command Authority makes policy. They certainly contribute to it. So, that's number one.

Senator TILLIS. But——

General KEANE. And I will say this——

Senator TILLIS. But, General Keane, could you imagine that they would be making their—the recommendations—I understand where the policy occurs, but they would be—recommendations that would lead the administration to this—the current policy, such as it is?

General KEANE. What happened here is—I think is very different than the process that we're—that many of us are used to experience when a President has made a decision that it's in his national interest to use military force to accomplish political objectives. He sort of—that is sort of stated to the Department of Defense, in terms of what his goals are, and then they would put together a campaign that would have various options and risk associated with it.

What happened on dealing with this issue, the—not only was the goal stated in terms of "defeat ISIS," but then the Pentagon was told many things in terms of what the parameters for that operation would be. And that is very different. In other words, "I don't want any civilians killed whatsoever." And many people pushed back on that and said, "That's impossible, Mr. President." But, the rules of engagement are so restrictive that we cannot conduct effective air operations to the degree that we know we can and keep people safe. "I don't want any boots on the ground." "But, can we put advisors down to help the units to—we need to train units and"—"No." So, those kind of restrictions are something I think most of us have not seen in our past, and how you make a policy and then provide the military instrument with a campaign plan and options associated with it. It's very different than our—what our experience is.

Senator TILLIS. Senator Reed, if I may ask just one other——

Senator REED. Please.

Senator TILLIS.—question.

And, you know, I think it's startling to hear someone who was formerly in command of NATO to say that it's at risk of dismantling. I think that that's a message that should be loud—heard loud and clear.

But, General Jones, you said something else that I'm personally very interested in, and it has to do with a highly effective nonlethal economic weapon that we're just keeping in the holster, and that has to do with aggressive energy policy, whether it's preventing the transportation cost of oil to go down through the Keystone Pipeline, whether it's preventing extraction of deposits that we have that can be economically extracted, whether it's preventing the long-term price of energy futures to be influenced by our ability and our resolve to extract through other methods, like hydraulic fracturing. Have we gotten in right on any measure, in terms of using energy policy to confront Russia's aggression?

General JONES. Senator, I do not believe that the United States has a strategic energy policy that anyone could read. And it's a little bit because of the way the Department of Energy was formed. Years and years ago, the Department of Energy was really the Department of Nuclear Energy. And in many ways, it still is.

I'm of the opinion that we have a great Secretary of Energy and a great Deputy. And I believe it would be wise for the President to designate the Secretary of Energy as the focal point for all energy, from coal to wind and everything in between, and that energy is now—energy security—international security—it's an international issue, and you—and because the United States has been able to, through its technology, and mostly its private sector, develop an astounding capability and capacity for energy for the future, in addition to our partners in Canada and also Mexico, that has changed the perception of what the American priorities are in the Middle East, for example. You know, the Middle East believes that energy is—energy for a security deal over the last 40 years is no longer viable, because we have our own energy. And, in fact, when you hear people talking about energy independence, I wince at that, because it does say, ''We've got ours. You're on your own.'' But, our energy good fortune can be used, and should be used, in the global playing field for developing countries and also as a response to what Mr. Putin is doing, and particularly in central and Eastern Europe.

And this plan that we're going to enter into the record today is a plan that will wean 14 nations off of Russian—from dependence on Russian energy. That's a staggering—if this works, this is a staggering response, an elegant response also, and an economic response, to Mr. Putin's actions.

Senator TILLIS. I look forward to seeing that.

Thank you, Mr. Chair.

Senator REED. Thank you, Senator Tillis.

In behalf of Chairman McCain, let me thank you all for extraordinary insightful testimony and for your commitment and dedication to the country over so many years.

Thank you.

The hearing is adjourned.

[Whereupon, at 12:15 p.m., the hearing was adjourned.]